Counties First

A House Divided

Restoring the Representative Government
Guaranteed to Every State
(Through a Convention of Counties)

By Matt Hawkins
Founder, Restoring Truth

Dedication

First, to my wife, who received a confirming answer for me to get civically involved in 2018, not knowing what was to come.

Second to my parents, to my dad Gordon, who was the consummate Boy Scout Leader in trying to instill in the minds of the youth, better concepts for what it means to be a good citizen; for my mother Gloria, who was civically involved within the community, and for both parents bridging conversations and supporting the moral fabric of a better America. They were examples of what it meant to be involved in strengthening others and in building a better America. Not to be overlooked, my Aunt Barbara and Cousin Tom, for recognizing the need for strong families and communities. For anyone that knows my family, if I fail to call out my own siblings, I will pay a price forever; to John for inspiring a love for history and books. Paul for instilling an awareness of love of duty, Peter for a love for humanity and civic engagement, Tim for sheer grit and determination, to accomplish the impossible, Sarah for her selfless support to lift and help others, Rebecca for her uncanny ability to recognize and understand trends, and Joe for his love for life and desire to find beauty in everything around him. Best of all for Joe, his faith to pursue what is needed, when the pathway ahead is not clear. While Joe is the youngest, he has continued to inspire since his passing several years ago. May his children always remember his example.

Third, thanks to the dedicated people that are choosing to be civically involved in bringing to light the abuses of government process, both intentional and not. One of the best Constitutionalists, G. R. Mobley, has been a dedicated servant in this cause of civic enlightenment. The fight to restore Transparency and Accountability includes too many people to be listed at this time, excepting for Loyd Hogan, who is a warrior on the front lines, always looking out for those that are overlooked and in trying to restore accountability.

In the past 10 years, I have noticed people from both sides of the political spectrum that are questioning how we got to where we are today. For anyone that has been involved in a business or personal life turnaround, what matters most is that we recognize we have a problem, then we take action as we identify the principles of truth that will set us on the right path.

This book is about identifying what we have done that is right, within our history, what we have done that is wrong, correcting, and in the process, we will make history that will be rewarding for generations to come.

Finally, I thank all who have engaged in the conversations that have allowed this idea for restoring county representation back into State Senates, to take hold. Thank you for a Providential God, that inspired the Founding Fathers to create a form and model of government, that is adaptable to all levels of governing, providing the simple guarantee that all government is to be Representative in Form. Just the same as God trusts we will be responsible in remembering where we receive our rights, "We the People" extend the trust, for which government is to serve the people, knowing that we reserve the right to clarify how the processes of government are to be administered. This book, describes a need for such clarification.

Truths to Consider

"All power is inherent in the people."

"The people retain a sovereign power
that precedes law—and law
must eventually reckon with it."

Government derives their rights from the people,
The people derive their rights from God.

**Consider the impact of NVIDIA on AI, then
Consider the impact that County representation
Can have on our future.**

You will find this and more inside.

*This is not a book
about just history,*

***It is about
the making of history.***

Foreword

A Republic, If You Can Keep It

At the close of the Constitutional Convention, Benjamin Franklin was asked what kind of government had been created. His answer was brief and cautionary: "A republic, if you can keep it."

For county officials, keeping a republic is not a philosophical concern. It is a practical one.

It appears in budget hearings where counties are required to implement state programs with little discretion. It appears in land-use decisions constrained by rules written far from the county itself. It appears when counties are charged with enforcing policies issued by state and federal agencies that will never bear responsibility for the results.

In these moments, the problem is not authority on paper. It is control in practice.

Counties are the level of government closest to the people. They conduct elections, maintain infrastructure, administer public health and safety, and respond first when emergencies arise. Yet over time, legislative and executive authority over these functions has steadily migrated upward—to state legislatures, Congress, and administrative bureaucracies—while counties have remained responsible for execution.

This migration did not occur through a single decision. It occurred incrementally, through statutes, regulations, funding conditions, and judicial interpretations that centralized decision-making while leaving implementation local. Counties retained obligations, but lost governing authority.

The result is a structural imbalance between county and state government—one that carries consequences beyond administrative efficiency. As authority moves farther from the people, the ability of individuals and communities to meaningfully govern themselves diminishes. What is lost is not merely local discretion, but a measure of personal and communal freedom rooted in self-government.

Policies affecting local conditions are increasingly decided far from the communities they govern. Counties are expected to comply and deliver results, but have limited ability to shape the rules under which they operate. Citizens experience this most acutely at the county level, where government is most visible yet influence is often weakest.

This book advances a clear argument: a republic cannot be kept if counties are reduced to administrative units rather than governing institutions, and the people cannot remain free when the decisions that govern their daily lives are made beyond their effective reach.

Restoring representative government therefore requires returning meaningful legislative and executive control to counties in matters that are inherently local. That restoration cannot be achieved through advisory bodies, informal coordination, or temporary reforms. It requires action.

A Convention of Counties, convened for a single and specific purpose, provides the lawful mechanism to do so.

Such a convention is not a permanent institution and not an alternative legislature. It is a constitutional event based on process within our U.S. Constitution, called to propose targeted clarification to governing policy. Its objective is to restore authority and control to the state's counties by constitutionally re-establishing their role as governing bodies, not merely administrative subdivisions.

Authority is restored not by the convention itself, but by the constitutional framework it produces. The convention performs its function and the counties govern, through Representation.

Under this approach, counties regain legislative and executive control over local affairs they already manage in practice—land use, local administration, enforcement priorities, and community governance—while the state retains authority over matters that are genuinely statewide in scope. The result is not fragmentation, but balance.

This reallocation strengthens all levels of government.

Counties regain the authority necessary to govern responsibly and transparently. States benefit from policies that reflect local conditions and are more effectively implemented. Citizens regain a closer connection between consent and governance—an essential condition for preserving both liberty and legitimacy in a representative republic.

Before outlining how such a convention can be structured and limited to this purpose, it is necessary to understand how counties lost this authority in the first place.

Chapter 1 examines the historical and institutional developments that led to the concentration of legislative and executive power at the state and federal levels, and how counties came to function primarily as administrators rather than constitutional participants in governance. That history provides the foundation for restoring what was promised—and for keeping the republic Franklin warned could be lost.

—Rodrigo Silveira

Disclaimer

The founding of America was built on the conversations of people in their churches, town squares and taverns. Today dialogue is found in social media, which seems to be the new Townsquare, through online communities and searches including the newest resource AI (for which I am proud to say that Grok and others have been tremendous library assistants), **but most importantly with people, for expanding the discussion.**

Source materials have been utilized where possible, and documented, to ensure that what is being represented is accurate. However, the author also realizes that he is the compiler of what has been read and discussed with others. As a result, there could be errors, for which we can correct with a discussion.

Errors or not, we all need to continue on our path for identifying Truth, as we work to build a society that improves and ensures Life, Liberty and the Pursuit of Happiness, for All. Like the Founders, 250 years ago, we are all allowed to have our opinions, with some opinions being better than others (lighten up). Through expanded discussions, we can better determine what is to be done, now.

Be a part of the discussion.

This book is about a solution

How we got to where we are today.
Why is the Constitution our solution.

**What you and I can do to correct the
progressive policies of our past.**

Better yet, how can counties be the solution to remedy our
National Debt, which is moving past $37 Trillion?

How can we be a part of history in the making,
for the benefit of future generations?

Contents

Part III: The Solution

Counties First

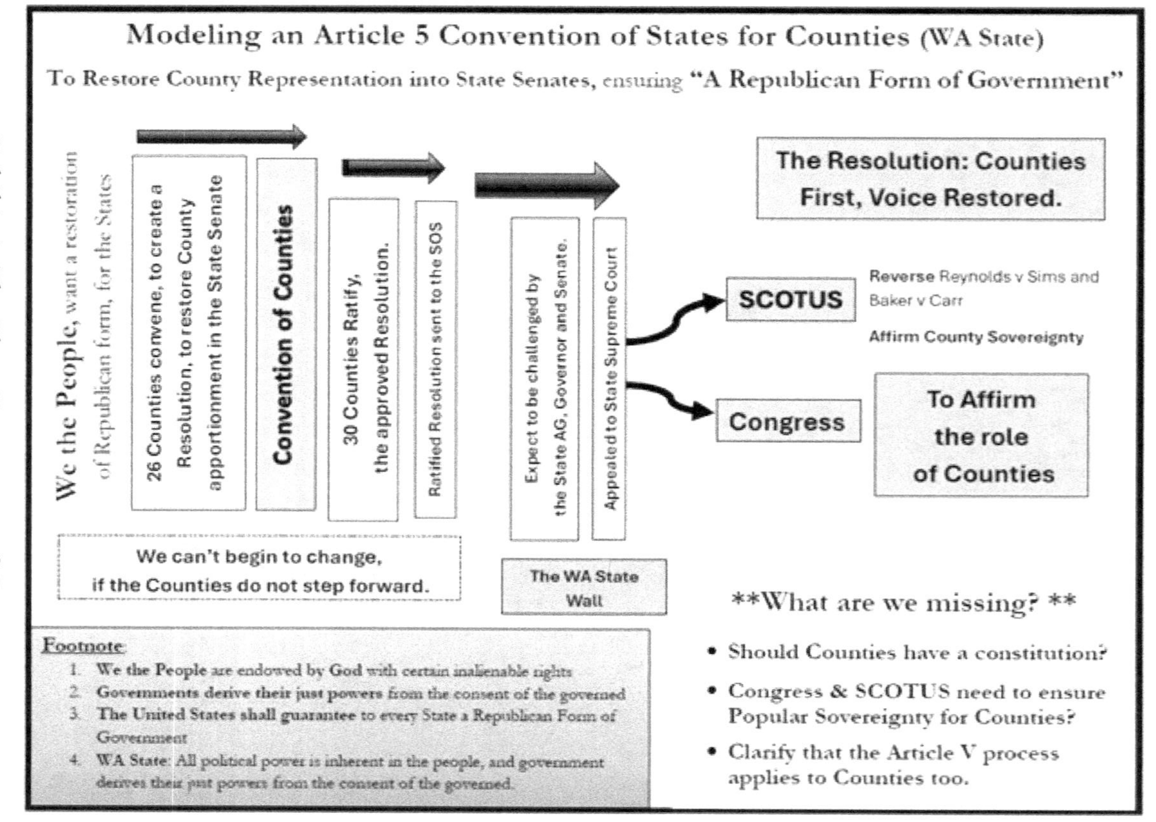

Exhibit-1, The Plan, Convention of Counties

Prologue

Three Times That Counties Drew the Line

Athens, Tennessee –1946

The returning veterans of McMinn County, Tennessee, had seen enough tyranny in Europe and the Pacific. They came home expecting to find the America they'd fought for.

Instead, they found Sheriff Paul Cantrell's machine: ballot-box stuffing, poll-tax scams, deputies beating voters, and a fee system that turned arrests into cash.

On election day **1946**, when a Black veteran named Tom Gillespie was pistol-whipped and shot for trying to vote and the deputies seized the ballot boxes, the GIs had had enough.

They broke into the National Guard armory, grabbed rifles, and laid siege to the jail where the ballots were hidden. The Battle of Athens lasted through the night. At dawn the Cantrell machine surrendered. The honest ballots were counted. The Veterans won.

One county drew a line in the dirt with rifles and dynamite.

America applauded. Hollywood may memorialize the event. And we all thought that was the last time citizens would ever have to fight their own government to protect a basic right, elections.

We were wrong.

Albany, Texas – 2024

Seventy-nine years later, in the packed courthouse of Shackelford County (population **3,265**), another group of citizens stood up.

County Judge John Viertel, called the meeting to order. The single agenda item: a resolution declaring that the southern border situation constitutes an "invasion" under Article I, Section 10 and Article IV, Section 4 of the U.S. Constitution, and that Shackelford County therefore possesses the sovereign authority to defend itself[1]

When the vote was called, all five commissioners raised their hands. Shackleford county showed unity and a backbone, as they joined the movement in Texas to take a stand against illegal immigration. What started out as a single county in the spring of **2021**, was now over **50** counties.

No shots were fired.
No dynamite was needed.
Because this time the weapon wasn't rifles.
It was the Constitution itself.

Since that February day, counties are taking stands, both for and against sanctuary policies on illegal immigration. They recognize a need to be involved in policy. They are waking up to the authority the Framers always intended them to have.

Adams County, Washington, 2025[2]

As a northern tier state combats the influx of illegal immigration, a rural county sheriff in Adams County Washington lends support to ICE, only to find that now the State Attorney General "AG" files a lawsuit. Key to the AG's argument, the sheriff was violating the "Keep Washington Working Act" that was enacted in **2019**.

So here we have a sheriff supporting his Constitutional oath of office, to support a federal government that is working to round-up the illegal immigrants that have invaded Adam's County. He is trying to support a safer community.

Maybe the Washington State problem is representative of a much larger problem of government process and how the mental health of state governments are becoming mentally confused. Perhaps this state of confusion, tilts towards what might be called **Münchausen by Olympia** (Olympia is the capital of Washington State).

In a state where illegal immigration spreads like a cancer, homelessness is recruited as though it is an industry to be expanded, youth transgender medicine & parental exclusion laws are being created against citizen input, an opioid and Fentanyl crisis is out of control, public safety is collapsing in our urban centers and spreading, the mental health crisis as evidenced by a behavioral-health bed shortage, the state continues to seek billions to fix the problems with no beneficial results, all while billions go missing, and lest we forget, wildfire season rings the bell of a forever climate emergency.

Yes the pattern for Münchausen by Olympia[3] is identical to **<u>Münchausen by proxy</u>**[4]:

- Exaggerate or actively worsen the condition of the "patient" (citizens).
- Punish effective local fixes that reduce state dependency (i.e. lawsuits and threats of funding cuts)
- Demand ever-larger payments and power for the caregiver because "the situation keeps getting worse."

That's **Münchausen by Olympia** in action. States are now evidencing a serious decline in their ability to govern. Why? **We have lost our representative form of government.**

This book is the story of how we got here — and the exact, peaceful, constitutional roadmap every county in America can use to finish what the veterans of McMinn County, the citizens of Shackelford County, and the sheriff of Adams County started and are supporting.

Because the Guarantee is still there.

Every State is guaranteed
a republican (representative)
form of government.

Which also **guarantees** that **locally we are guaranteed a representative form of government.**
And this time, We the People are going to enforce it.

> "To subject local communities to the political whims of state governors ... poses a manifest danger to the republic."
> **Paul R. DeHart**
> **Ronald J. Oakerson**

Part I

The Promise

Chapter 1

The Forgotten Guarantee
Everybody Forgot Was There

"The United States shall guarantee to every State in this Union a
Republican Form of Government…"
— **Article IV, Section 4, U.S. Constitution**

If you went to public school after about **1975**, there is a **99**% chance nobody ever told you what those fifteen words actually meant as they were written in **1787**.

They did not mean "no kings."

They did not mean "democracy."

They **did NOT** give reference to a "political party".

And they most certainly did not mean "whatever the Supreme Court feels like this decade."

They meant one thing, and one thing only:

*Our Model or Republican Form of Government is the United States Congress — one house apportioned by population, the other apportioned by fixed geography so that regardless of your living in an urban or rural community, your voice could **not be gerrymandered away**.*

In **1787,** that fixed geography for the States, was the county (parishes and so forth).

For **177** years, the county remained a building block to good government.

Then, in a single decade (with decisions in **1962–1964**), nine men in black robes erased it with the stroke of a pen.

This chapter is the receipt.

The Day the Founders Put Counties in Charge of the States

When the Constitutional Convention deadlocked in the summer of **1787**, the argument was never about whether big states should dominate small ones. The argument was about whether population should be allowed to dominate over geography at all. The question that was asked then and that needs to be understood now, ***how do we ensure a representative form of government?***

To understand the issues dealing with governance, consider what we learned about representative government during the times of "**The Articles of Confederation**" or "**AoC**" (**1781-1789**).

1) The **AoC** were **ratified by representative, not popular vote**
    a. This followed the model of early colonial charters, early state constitutions and treaties.
    b. State ratifying conventions were different from legislatures
2) **Ratification required 100% support**, by all states[5]
    a. In each instance this ratification was done by state legislative action after county input
3) **The federal legislative body, was to be a unicameral legislature** (single body, called the '**Congress of the Confederation**'
    a. ***No executive branch***
    b. ***No judicial branch***, *the judiciary powers were within the Congress*

Contrast with the U.S. Constitution (**1789** to **present**)
- The **Legislature**, is **bicameral** (House + Senate)

- **Legislature Representation**, state equality with
- Population apportionment (**House**) + State equality by fixed geography (**Senate**)
- **Executive**, to be a President
- **Judiciary**, Supreme Court + lower courts, as agreed to by Congress and States
- **Bill of Rights,** to further guarantee rights to the people

Roger Sherman and Oliver Ellsworth of Connecticut proposed the deal that saved the Convention: representation by population in the House, representation by equal suffrage for states in the Senate. Every schoolchild learns that part.

"Once delegates established equal representation in the Senate, they needed to determine how many senators would represent each state. State constitutions offered some guidance. Several states designated one senator per county or district, while in Delaware there were three senators for each of the three counties."

The Records of the Federal Convention of 1787[6]

What almost no one learns is that the exact same compromise was immediately copied downward to the states themselves.

By **1790, 10** of the original **13** states adapted to a bicameral system (**Georgia** transitioned in **1789, Pennsylvania** and **Rhode Island** in **1790**). Vermont which was added as the 14th state, believed that simplicity would be served with a unicameral legislature operating as a "General Assembly" in 1791, then switched to a bicameral legislature in 1836

- All other new states entering the Union modeled the bicameral process:

- **Lower house** → apportioned by population (sometimes with a one-representative-per-county floor)
- **Upper house** → one or two senators per county, parish, or district — almost always the county
- That wasn't an accident. That was **the Guarantee Clause**[7] doing its job.

The Guarantee Clause in Action — Three Snapshots
1. **Virginia 1788** ratification convention. The official vote to ratify the new Constitution was taken not by popular ballot, but by county as the representative county votes were then aggregated into the State legislature. Counties cast the deciding votes, exactly the way states would cast the deciding votes in the U.S. Senate.
2. **Washington Territory 1878** Constitution (the one Congress rejected, primarily because of the national politics of the day, and the fact that an Enabling Act by Congress had not been passed yet.)

By the time of the **1889** state constitution being written, we find that Article II, Section 6 states: *"…no representative district shall be divided in the formation of a senatorial district."*

Translation: county lines were locked in stone for the senate. Population could shift all it wanted; the senate map did not move.

Senator Everett Dirksen's warning on **the Senate floor, (1964)**

As a clear proponent for reversing the SCOTUS decision of Reynolds v Sims, Senator Dirksen provided clarity as he understood the clear and distinct role the House and Senate played in representing the interests of the people. He also understood the need for checks & balances within the system of government. No wonder then that he was a proponent for ensuring that State Senates should be represented by the interests of counties.[8]

If he were alive today, perhaps Senator Dirksen would still suggest, in relation to the effort to restore the voice of counties back into the state senate, through a Convention of Counties, that *"stronger than all the armies is an idea whose time has come… it will not be stayed or denied, **it is here**."*

Senator Dirksen, from Illinois, almost saved us. His amendment to overturn Reynolds v. Sims fell seven votes short of the two-thirds needed

Today we can take action.

What "Republican Form" Actually Looked Like on the Ground

- **1790**: While **3** of the original **13** states, followed a unicameral system of legislation, initially, they each quickly adapted a bicameral process, modeling the Republican Form in the U.S. Constitution.
- **1800**: All states except **Vermont** (which transitioned in **1836**) modeled their state senate seats into Bicameral legislative bodies.
- As a side note, **Rhode Island** moved to a Bicameral system in **1696**, just **33** years after their original charter by the crown in **1663**. Remember also that this was the last state to ratify the U.S. Constitution and did so by the narrowest of margins. Read Madisons arguments in **Federalist #62** & **#63**[9], regarding the necessity, stability and wisdom of a senate. Then in **1843**, Rhode Island agreed to a formal constitutional structure by approving a new state constitution which included a bicameral legislature, which further validates the universal support for bicameralism.
- **1920**: In a Brennan Center for Justice report

"Apportionment of State Legislatures, **1776-1920**", authors Douglas Keith and Eric Petry state on page **1**, that "**75%** of state legislative chambers were apportioned on the basis of population – albeit often with **minimum representation provisions for counties**, with the majority of the rest (usually upper houses-*senates*) apportioned on the basis of fixed districts (***Counties***)". [10]

- **1950**: We find that the county influence on apportionment within the State Senates was still very strong. Even as Alaska and Hawaii were added, the use of counties was modified to regions within Alaska and islands in Hawaii.

However, the idea of population influence on state senate's began to be influenced as early as **1803**, as states began to take a nod for recognizing some level of population apportionment to counties.

Yet the 13 original states adhered to clear alignment to county boundaries. Was it the Progressive policies following the Civil War that had a great influence on these actions? Perhaps as new states were admitted, Congress created a bias. Congress gave instructions that seemed to pave the way to move away from Representative government.

		State Senate's-Representation			Today
Phase	State	Admitted	1791-1964	Population Influence	1 Person 1 Vote
Wave 1 (Pre-Civil War)	Delaware	7 Dec 1787	County Based	No	*Population Based*
	Pennsylvania	12 Dec 1787	County Based	No	*Population Based*
	New Jersey	18 Dec 1787	County Based	No	*Population Based*
	Georgia	2 Jan 1788	County Based	No	*Population Based*
	Connecticut	9 Jan 1788	County Based	No	*Population Based*
	Massachusetts	6 Feb 1788	Counties & Towns	No	*Population Based*
	Maryland	28 Apr 1788	County based	No	*Population Based*
	South Carolina	23 May 1788	County Based	No	*Population Based*
	New Hampshire	21 Jun 1788	County Based	No	*Population Based*
	Virginia	25 Jun 1788	County Based	No	*Population Based*
	New York	26 Jul 1788	County based	No	*Population Based*
	North Carolina	21 Nov 1789	County Based	No	*Population Based*
	Rhode Island	29 May 1790	Counties	No	*Population Based*
	Vermont	4 Mar 1791	County Based	No	*Population Based*
	Kentucky	1 Jun 1792	County Based	No	*Population Based*
	Tennessee	1 Jun 1796	County Based	No	*Population Based*
Wave 2 (Pre-Civil War)	Ohio	1 Mar 1803	County Based	Yes	*Population Based*
	Louisiana	30 Apr 1812	County Based (Parishes)	No	*Population Based*
	Indiana	11 Dec 1816	County Based	Yes	*Population Based*
	Mississippi	10 Dec 1817	County Based	No	*Population Based*
	Illinois	3 Dec 1818	County Based	Yes	*Population Based*
	Alabama	14 Dec 1819	County Based	No	*Population Based*
	Maine	15 Mar 1820	Counties & Towns	Yes	*Population Based*
	Missouri	10 Aug 1821	County Based	No	*Population Based*
	Arkansas	15 Jun 1836	County Based	No	*Population Based*
	Michigan	26 Jan 1837	County Based	Yes	*Population Based*
	Florida	3 Mar 1845	County Based	No	*Population Based*
	Texas	29 Dec 1845	County Based	Yes	*Population Based*
	Iowa	28 Dec 1846	County Based	Yes	*Population Based*
	Wisconsin	29 May 1848	County Based	Yes	*Population Based*
	California	9 Sep 1850	County Based	Yes	*Population Based*
	Minnesota	11 May 1858	County Based	Yes	*Population Based*
	Oregon	14 Feb 1859	County Based	Yes	*Population Based*
Wave 3 (Civil War to Post Civil War)	Kansas	29 Jan 1861	County Based	Yes	*Population Based*
	West Virginia	20 Jun 1863	County Based	No	*Population Based*
	Nevada	31 Oct 1864	County Based	No	*Population Based*
	Nebraska	1 Mar 1867	County Based	Yes	*Population Based*
	Colorado	1 Aug 1876	County Based	No	*Population Based*
	North Dakota	2 Nov 1889	County Based	Yes	*Population Based*
	South Dakota	2 Nov 1889	County Based	No	*Population Based*
	Montana	8 Nov 1889	County Based	No	*Population Based*
	Washington	11 Nov 1889	County Based	Yes	*Population Based*
	Idaho	3 Jul 1890	County Based	No	*Population Based*
	Wyoming	10 Jul 1890	County Based	No	*Population Based*
	Utah	4-Jan-1896	County Based	Yes	*Population Based*
Wave 4 1900's	Oklahoma	16-Nov-1907	County Based	Yes	*Population Based*
	New Mexico	6-Jan-1912	County Based	Yes	*Population Based*
	Arizona	14-Feb-1912	County Based	Yes	*Population Based*
	Alaska	3-Jan-1959	Region Based	Yes	*Population Based*
	Hawaii	21-Aug-1959	Island Based	Yes	*Population Based*

Exhibit-2, County based State Senate's

1964: **Reynolds v. Sims** — **0** of **50** (*None of the states senates are allowed to align by boundaries alone, population is to be the main determining factor,* **1 person, 1 vote**)

The SCOTUS decisions out of the Warren Court are very clear with the intention of mandating the progressive policy of representation by population as opposed to fixed boundaries or counties. All state senates will now be apportioned by population. In most instances the senate districts are now identical to the representative state districts. SCOTUS's decision resulted in a ***pseudo-bicameral legislature for states***. Pseudo, in the sense that the state senate was now in most instances representing the same electing population as the house, <u>*with boundaries not being fixed,*</u> **but subject to gerrymandering.**

The gerrymandering now opened opportunities for urban centers within a state to control all political outcomes. Rural counties lost their voice. This decision alone, would now put states on a collision course with the federal government as one is now a pure "democracy form" and the other a clear "representative form" of government. Remember that a democracy only protects the interests of the majority, while a representative ensures the interests of the minority are protected.

The judicial coup was total.

The One Justice Who Saw It Coming

Justice John Marshall Harlan II (grandson of the great dissenter in Plessy v. Ferguson) wrote the dissent in Reynolds v. Sims[11]. His belief was that the Constitution does not grant unlimited power to revise or dictate the political framework of the states.

"The Court's action now bringing them [state legislative apportionments] within the purview of the Fourteenth Amendment **amounts to nothing less than an exercise of the amending power by this Court."**

Which the court does not have, *only the States can*

amend.

"This Court, limited in function in accordance with that premise, does not serve its high purpose when it exceeds its authority, even to satisfy justified impatience with the slow workings of the political process. For when, in the name of constitutional interpretation, the Court adds something to the Constitution that was deliberately excluded from it, the Court in reality substitutes its view of what should be so for the amending process."

We the People have a right to correct the abuse.

"What is done today deepens my conviction that judicial entry into this realm is profoundly ill-advised and constitutionally impermissible."

"So far as the Federal Constitution is concerned, the complaints in these cases should all have been dismissed below for failure to state a cause of action, because what has been alleged or proved shows no violation of any constitutional right."

Justice Harlan was correct.

"The consequence of today's decision is that... the local District Court or, it may be, the state courts, are given blanket authority and the constitutional duty to supervise apportionment of the State Legislatures. It is difficult to imagine a more intolerable and inappropriate interference by the judiciary with the independent legislatures of the States."

Stated differently, we are relying on a Judicial Form of Government, not what we were guaranteed, *"A Republican Form of Government."*

"Had the Court paused to probe more deeply into the matter, it would have found that the Equal Protection Clause was

never intended to inhibit the States in choosing any democratic method they pleased for the apportionment of their legislatures."

"These decisions also cut deeply into the fabric of our federalism... the aftermath of these cases... will have been achieved at the cost of a radical alteration in the relationship between the States and the Federal Government, more particularly the Federal Judiciary."

In short, actions by SCOTUS in the apportionment of state legislative bodies have ensured a conflict now between States and the Federal body of government. [12]

He lost 8–1.

But he was right.

And the proof is in the pudding: every single problem the county movement is fighting today — gun controls passed in the dead of night, runaway taxes, school boards captured by teachers' unions, open borders enforced by sanctuary cities — every single one of them became politically possible after rural counties lost their representation in state government through a means of the judicial-gerrymandering of ALL state governments.

Simply, creating a pseudo-bicameral system of government, has allowed for the Judiciary to restore an inferior means of governing to what we had during the Articles of Confederation, and worse, setting the stage for further nullifying the voice of Counties. Our states urban centers are on the pathway to majority control, the same as we find in our global socialist and communist countries.

The Guarantee Is Still There

Article IV, Section 4, has never been amended.

It has never been repealed.

It has never even been re-interpreted by constitutional convention.

It is still the supreme law of the land.

And the only institution that has the raw constitutional authority to enforce it against a runaway Court is the one the Framers created for exactly that purpose:

We the People, acting through the sovereign political communities closest to us — our counties. This is "**Popular Sovereignty**" in action.

The rest of this book is the roadmap, to correction. But first:

To understand our evolution as a country, take time to compare

- *how American governing systems have evolved,*
- *and how businesses in the free markets adapt to market conditions.*

The American Experiment as Product Development:

From Alpha to Gold Standard

"It is impossible to improve any process until it is standardized."
— Masaaki Imai, Kaizen

The U.S. Constitution was the creation of a standard for process, in representative government. The Constitution is not what we started with, but what we acquired after study, deliberation and testing.

Think of the United States or its Constitution, not as a static document, but as a **product** — the most successful governance platform in history. Like any great tech product, it went through rigorous iterations, testing, and continuous improvement. And like any product, it can be **regressed** by bad updates.

Contrasting a Technology Evolution and how The United States of America, came into existence.

Exhibit-3

"Slack" The evolution of "Slack" as gaming product to Messaging App (2009-2021)	**"The United States of America"** The evolution from Exploring new trade routes to Creation of a Nation. (1492-1800)
The Product: Slack was conceived as a whimsical online game, only to pivot through market dynamics, from a failed launch to a $28-M acquisition by **Sales Force**.	**The Product:** Christopher Columbus took on the challenge, in 1492, to identify new trade routes, believing that his new idea had merit. Over 284 years, trade routes gave birth to a new nation, "The United States of America".
The Idea: in 2009, a small group assembled to create "Tiny Speck", a startup focused on a multiplayer online role-playing game called Glitch. While the game was core to the experience, the team members created an internal communication tool for collaboration and internal communication. The Chat tool was a side utility and not even being considered for commercialization.	**The Idea:** Once Columbus moved forward with his initial thought, he learned that he had opened up something new, which pivoted in the early 1600's to something entirely new, settlements for purposes of profit and expansion, mixed in with religious freedom. The Product was evolving into a variety of ideas and possibilities, as both economic and environmental conditions encouraged the product to evolve.

Alpha Release: occurred in 2010-2011, as a small group of users were invited in to play and test the games mechanics and stability. Feedback was good, but scalability issues surfaced, with Server costs being high and user retention low. The internal chat tool evolved as features like searchable archives were added and integrations to handle the team's growing needs. This phase also exposed the "bugs": it was too niche, struggling to attract a broad audience amid competition for other Multi-player role playing games like World of Warcraft.	**Alpha Release:** (1620's to 1750's): The alpha release for the new world adapted easily amongst the 13 colonies by the early to mid-1700's as each colony adapted. Virginia focused on the economics of Tobacco; Massachusetts focused on Puritan theocracy as they extended into community covenants; Pennsylvania introduced Quaker tolerance. Within these models we saw elements of indentured servitude and chattel slavery which shared a "core dependency" with southern economies. Conflicts arose as seen with King Philip's war in 1675 and Bacon's Rebellion in 1676, which exposed scalability issues in class and racial tensions. Population growth from 250-k in 1700 to over 2-M in 1770 showed that the product-market fit, but that the integration was clunky—less cohesion and simply regional silos.

Beta Testing: Game launch and the looming Pivot (2011-2012). Glitch hit public beta in March 2011 and fully launched in September 2011. The graphics were polished, social quests existed, and monetization via in-game purchase. Problem, engagement plateaued; despite a dedicated fanbase, it couldn't scale profitability. Tiny Speck shut down Glitch in December 2012, citing unsustainable costs and market fit issues. This failure forced a hard pivot: the team recognized that their internal chat tool, now battle tested from years of use, had more potential than the game itself. Within weeks, they repurposed it into a standalone product, stripping game specific elements and focusing on workplace communication. The original gaming idea had morphed completely into an enterprise messaging app by this point, emphasizing real-time collaboration, integrations (e.g. with Google Drive), and searchability—features absent from email or basic chat apps like HipChat.	**Beta Testing:** A semi-cohesive system from 1750's to 1776. This semi-cohesive system continued to build, as friction with British "Stakeholders" intensified. The French and Indian War (1754-1763) acted as a load test with the expanding territory while racking up debt, leading to "feature creep" like the Stamp Act (1765) and the Townshend Acts (1767), all unwanted taxes that sparked user backlash such as the Boston Tea Party in 1773. Beta users (colonists) formed feedback groups like the Sons of Liberty and Committees of Correspondence, demanding more autonomy. This phase highlighted bugs: and over-reliance on British imports, weak intercolonial coordination, and ideological divides (loyalists vs Patriots). The product was viable but needed a pivot—enter the Continental Congresses (1774-1775) as beta review sessions.

Release Candidate (RC): Slacks Preview and Refinement (2013) Renamed Slack "Searchable Log of All Conversation and Knowledge", the product entered a private beta in February 2013, inviting select companies to test it. This RC phase focused on ironing out usability, adding channels for organized discussions, and an emoji reaction for fun. User feedback led to quick iteration, like better mobile support. By August 2013, a public preview (essentially an open beta) launched, attracting thousands of teams. The pivot was complete, what started as a game dev tool, was now a polished alternative to fragmented office communication.	**Release Candidate (RC):** The Launch of Independence and War, debugging (1776-1783). The Declaration of Independence in 1776 marked the RC phase. This was a bold fork from the British codebase, proclaiming "life, liberty, and the pursuit of happiness" as core features. The Revolutionary War (1775-1783) was live testing under fire—battles like Saratoga (1777) validated alliance (e.g. with France), while Valley Forge (1777-1778) exposed chain vulnerabilities. By the Treaty of Paris (1783), the RC passed certification: independence achieved, but with known issues like war debt and territorial disputes. This wasn't a full release yet, just proof that the product could stand alone.

V1.0: Official Launch and Market Fit (2014) Slack v1.0 officially launched in February 2014, with core features like threaded conversation, file sharing and third-party app integrations. It exploded in popularity, hitting 1 million daily active users by 2015. This version solidified Slack as a "Completely different" product from Glitch—no gaming elements remained, replaced by productivity tools. Early adopters praised their intuitiveness, but scalability bugs (e.g. message limits) prompted patches.	**V1.0:** Articles of Confederation—The buggy first launch (1781-1789). Launched in 1781, V1.0 was the initial public release: a loose alliance of states with a weak central "server" (no executive branch, no taxation power). Features included state sovereignty and a unicameral Federal Congress, but crashes were frequent –Shays Rebellion (1786-1787) highlighted security flaws in handling internal unrest. Economic modules like interstate trade were fragmented, leading to calls for an upgrade, this version needed to adapt with a need to prioritize a centralized government if stability was to be ensured.

V2.0 Beta: Enterprise Push and Feature Expansion (2016-2017) By the beta stage of what is considered v2.0, Slack had morphed further into an enterprise-grade platform. The beta test advanced features like shared channels for cross-country collaboration, voice/video calls, and enhanced security. This iteration addressed feedback from larger organizations, pivoting from a fun, startup-focused chat app to a robust tool competing with Microsoft Teams. Bugs like notification overload were debugged, and integrations expanded to over 1,500 apps. By full v2.0 rollout, Slack was no longer just messaging—it was a "hub" for work, with AI-assisted search in beta testing.	V2.0 The Constitution—major rewrite and stability. (1789-1800). The Constitutional Convention (1787) was a full refactor, resulting in V2.0: a federal system with separation of powers, checks and balances, and a stronger executive. Ratified in 1788 and operational by 1789, it included features like the Electoral College and Bicameral Legislature. Early patches followed with the Bill of Rights (1791) as V2.1, added user protections like free speech to address anti-Federalist feedback. Under George Washington's presidency (1789-1797) the product stabilized handling "bugs" like the Whiskey Rebellion (1794) and establishing institutions via the Judiciary act (1789). By John Adams's term (1797-1801), V2.0 faced stress from foreign affairs (XYZ Affair, 1797-1798) and internal divides (Alien and Sedition Acts, 1798) but this all proved scalable. By 1800, with Thomas Jefferson's election, the core architecture was set for future expansion like westward growth.

V3.0: AI Integration and Ecosystem Maturity (2018-2019) V3.0 equivalents emerged around 2018-2019 with major overhauls, including Workflow Builder (2019) for custom automation and deeper AI features like suggested replies. The product had indeed evolved from a simple chat to an intelligent collaboration suite, incorporating machine learning for productivity insights.	America's "development" was iterative and messy, driven by crises as much as vision: From a speculative idea to a robust V2.0, it evolved through trial and error, much like software facing real-world users.

So why the comparison. In everyday life we find that success is normally not just a casual experience, but one that is built on the foundation of following good process and adapting within constraints. As humans, we adapt and grow daily.

One central feature in the evolution of America was in the adherence to respect by the Founding Fathers, and of the Founding Fathers as to the unique features and contributions of each of the **13** colonies, as they became States. This was core to supporting the agreement to move from a model of a Unicameral to a Bicameral Congress. Concurrently our Founding Fathers saw fit to clearly ***provide a Guarantee***, that "*The United States **shall guarantee to every State** in this Union a Republican Form of Government*".

This guarantee was not designed to ensure that only the Federal body of government was to be "Republican in Form", but that each State would be afforded the same right. Meaning that this form, as agreed to at a federal level, was to be modeled at the State level. How do we know, review the examples of the formation of the State legislative bodies, as they ratified the Constitution. Only **3** States operated with Unicameral Legislatures, the remaining **10** had already adopted Bicameral Legislative bodies. Quickly all states adapted Bicameral systems, with future states to follow, **as they followed "form".**

Continuous Improvement

Another argument for respecting good forms and processes. Consider the idea of "Continuous Improvement". We find in manufacturing; efficiency is built upon following great processes and in respecting the idea of continuous improvement. ISO Certifications have improved profitability by improving the quality of output and streamlining production. Apparently in the Free Markets, ISO and Continuous Improvement are respected and valued as a universal truth.

> **W. Edwards Deming** suggests *"A system is a network of interdependent components that work together to try to accomplish the aim of the system. A system must have an aim. Without an aim, there is no system."*

The aim for America, under a Representative Republic form of Government:

> *Confidence in the idea that Government is a servant of the people, that elections are transparent and reliable, that we promote the ideals of our Declaration of Independence and U.S. Constitution.*

We want there to be a preservation of propety rights, for an adherence to U.S. Constitutional law and order, a respect for one to practice their religion, and any other rights that we choose to declare in our Bill of Rights. Again simply, that We the People are expected to assume responsibilities for our outcome, by respecting all tenants of what we have inherited.

Masaaki Imai *states: "It is impossible to improve any process until it is standardized. If the process is shifting from here to there, then any improvement will just be one more variation that is occasionally used and mostly ignored. One must standardize, and thus stabilize the process, before continuous improvement can be made."*

This idea to standardize is inherent in the creation of "Forms" or processes.

> *"The one pervading evil of democracy is the tyranny of the majority, or rather of that party, not always the majority, that succeeds, by force or fraud, in carrying elections."*
> **—Lord Acton**

Our significant iterations occurred as we moved from the Articles of Confederation to the U.S. Constitution. These iterations on Form of Government included stability. That is until the **1960's** when a Progressive Supreme Court of the United States "SCOTUS", decided to follow the pathway of pure Democracy for our States. *This is one of the major problems we need to root out, and restore, so that we can return to the Guarantee of a Republican Form of government for our States.*

The same as in good product development, recognize the iterations of our own system of government, as we moved through each phase of development. We moved from a Unicameral body to Bicameral, from a choice to rule by majority to balancing with Representative bodies of government, both locally, within our States and Nationally. ***Why*** *would we even consider then moving backwards and reverting to simple Democracies wherein only the majority rules, at the risk of subjecting the minority to forms of Servitude?*

> "In a democracy, the majority
> of the citizens is capable of
> exercising the most cruel
> oppressions upon the minority."
> — **Edmund Burke**

"Evolution and Regression" of Americas governing system

	Evolution and Regression of Americas governing system		
Phase	**Year**	**"Product Version"**	**Key Pivot Point**
Alpha	1776-1781	Declaration of Independence & Articles of Confederation	Unicameral, weak central government, crashed under Shays' Rebellion
Beta	1781-1787	Confederation 2.0	Still too weak. States ignored Congress.
1.0 Launch	1787-1789	U.S. Constitution	Bicameral federal + county based state senates. Passed the QA (ratification)
1.1-1.9	1791-1868	Bill of Rights & 14th Amendment	Bug Fixes. Guarantee Clause enforced. States ship with county senates.
Gold Standard	1868-1950	Post-Dillon stability	Most states retain fixed-geography senates. ISO certified durability.
Disastrous Regression	1962-1964	Reynolds v Sims	SCOTUS force installs "Democracy OS" no states retain county senates.
Restore Representation	2026- ?	Convention of Counties	Counties demand to revert to 1.1. This book is the patch.

Exhibit-4

W. Edwards Deming (the father of modern quality control) said: *"A system must have an aim. Without an aim, there is no system."*

The aim of the American product? **Secure the blessings of liberty to ourselves and our posterity** — via a **republican form** that balances population and geography. Then, by example, shine our light so that others might follow.

The **1964** "update" violated every principle of good engineering:
- **Removed** the firewall (county senates)
- **Introduced** single-point failure (urban supermajorities)
- **Ignored** user feedback (rural counties)
- **Restored a failed model** from the Articles of Confederation.

Just as no aerospace firm would revert from titanium to tin, no representative republic should revert from bicameral representation to a unicameral democracy, especially through judicial action. A representative form of government requires that the people understand and value the benefits of representative votes over what we have been led to believe, which has been to value a strict adherence to popular votes. We are being lead down the wrong pathway.

ISO 9001 demands standardization before improvement. The Framers gave us the standard. Reynolds broke it.

We are the QA team.

And with the Convention of Counties, we want to roll back to the last well-known configuration we had, to the standards **proscribed by the original 13 States**, with county representation in our state senates. More importantly, we want to align more closely to **Cooley's Doctrine** and away from **Dillon's Law**. In any event, **we want clarity for the sovereignty of We the People** and **our Counties.**

Chapter 2

Counties as the Parents of States
From Territories to Enabling Acts

There is only **one guarantee, clearly stated** within the U.S. Constitution, which is:

"The United States shall guarantee to every State in this Union a Republican Form of Government..."

(Article IV, Section 4)

Then within the Bill of Rights, we have the further qualifier that:

*"The powers not delegated to the United States by the Constitution, nor prohibited by it to the States, are reserved to the States respectively, **or to the people.**"*

— Tenth Amendment, U.S. Constitution

The clear stipulation is that we have enumerated rights being granted upon the federal body of government, that other rights are to be conferred onto the States, and finally that **"the people"** are to **retain ALL other rights.**

If states are the parents of the federal union, then the federal body must be the child. **Who then created the states?**

The original **13** states started as colonial charters issued by the King of England, later we find that the subsequent enabling acts of the U.S. Congress both embodied the principle of popular sovereignty—a foundational truth articulated by the Founding

Fathers, wherein ultimate political authority resides in "We the People," enabling them to create and structure governments from the ground up. This approach, predating the restrictive **Dillon's Rule** of the late **19th** century, aligned with the inherent right of local self-government as championed in **Thomas Cooley's Doctrine**, which rooted local autonomy in Anglo-Saxon traditions and the people's sovereign consent, rather than mere grants from higher authority. Echoing the Founders' vision, as seen in James Madison's defense of federalism where states and localities retain *sovereignty derived from the people*, these instruments facilitated a layered governance: starting with local entities like towns or counties, ascending to colonial or state structures, and ultimately forming a national union.

What really occurred with the granting of the Colonial Charters, unbeknownst to the king, was a reinforcement of the idea that the people were really the sovereign agents. This concept laid the groundwork for and expressed itself again as Enabling Acts created territories and allowed for the states to be created.

Colonial Charters in practice empowered settlers to exercise popular sovereignty by establishing colonies as self-organizing communities. The Virginia Charter of **1606** and Massachusetts Bay Charter of **1629**, for instance, vested authority in the people through company assemblies or freemen's elections, allowing inhabitants to form governments consonant with English liberties but adapted to local needs. This reflected the Founders' later emphasis, as in the Declaration of Independence, that governments derive "just powers from the consent of the governed," with charters serving as vehicles for the people to claim and structure their own rule in new lands. Cooley's Doctrine would later formalize this as an inherent right, predating Dillon's narrow view by drawing on these early practices where local sovereignty was not delegated but intrinsic to the people's will.[13]

Enabling acts mirrored this by authorizing territorial inhabitants to convene and draft constitutions, often assembled through county representation, embodying the people's sovereign act of self-creation. The **Enabling Act of 1802** for Ohio, building on the Northwest Ordinance's republican guarantees, enabled *"We the People"* of the territory to form a state government, with Congress's role merely facilitative rather than originative—aligning with Cooley's insistence on local self-government as a constitutional norm rooted in popular sovereignty. Founders like **Thomas Jefferson** *viewed such processes as extensions of local civic duty, where sovereignty flows upward from communities to states and the nation.*[14]

Layered Governance built from local foundations

Under charters, popular sovereignty manifested in the creation of towns as primary seats of self-rule, where inhabitants elected officials and managed affairs, layering into broader colonial assemblies. In Massachusetts, for example, towns like Boston became crucibles of local democracy, prefiguring the Founders' republicanism where power ascends from the people through nested structures—town to colony to (eventually) nation—without needing perpetual royal fiat. This bottom-up dynamic aligned with Cooley's vision of localities as inherently self-governing, immune to arbitrary higher interference, and echoed Madison's federalist balance where local entities safeguard popular liberty.

Enabling acts extended this by enabling the formation of counties as local governments within emerging territories, where the people's delegates organized seats of justice and administration. Acts like those of **1889** for the Dakotas or **1906** for Oklahoma empowered territorial citizens to subdivide into counties, preparing for a hierarchy from local to state to federal levels—all grounded in the sovereign people's consent, as per Cooley's Doctrine and the Founders' dual sovereignty model. This predated Dillon's Rule by treating local units as organic expressions of popular will, not mere creatures of state legislatures.[15]

A Model to Safeguard Rights and Civic Participation

Both the Charters and the Enabling Acts included provisions affirming the people's sovereign rights, such as charters' extension of Englishmen's liberties and enabling acts' mandates for republican forms, eventually to be free from slavery. These ensured that local governments, as the closest to the people, protected inherent freedoms, aligning with Cooley's emphasis on local self-government as a bulwark against centralized overreach and the Founders' view of popular sovereignty demanding active civic responsibility. Land grants in both supported settlement and education, empowering communities to build sustainable self-rule.

In essence, charters and enabling acts were not top-down impositions but enablers of popular sovereignty, allowing "We the People" to forge governments starting locally—through towns and counties—and scaling to states and nation, in harmony with Cooley's inherent rights doctrine and the Founding Fathers' republican framework for governance.[16]

Building upon the foundational role of colonial charters and enabling acts as enablers of popular sovereignty—where "We the People" inherently possess the right to form layered governments from local units upward—this clarification extends the discussion to the U.S. Constitution's implicit recognition of counties (or equivalent local entities like parishes) as essential building blocks of representative governance. Aligning with Cooley's Doctrine, which suggests local self-government as an inherent, pre-existing right derived from the people's consent rather than a mere legislative grant, and the Founding Fathers' emphasis on republican structures where power ascends from grassroots communities, the Constitution's design reflects this bottom-up sovereignty. While counties are not explicitly named, their role in facilitating representative forms of government underscores the people's authority to check higher levels through local mechanisms, predating Dillon's Rule's top-down constraints.[17]

The Constitution's Emphasis on "People" and "Representatives" in a Representative "Form" of Government.

The Constitution references 'people' **11** times (often as "the people" or "We the People", emphasizing collective sovereignty) and "representative(s)" **10** times highlighting the people's role in electing representatives to form governments. Notably, **"form" appears twice:** in the Preamble ("*form a more perfect Union*") and Article IV, Section 4 ("*Republican Form of Government*"), underscoring the Founders' focus on structures that enable self-rule without needing to enumerate every local unit like counties. This silence on counties is insignificant, as the document prioritizes the inherent rights of "The People" to safeguard and establish representative systems, echoing Jeferson's and Madison's views that sovereignty originates from individuals and communities, scaling up to states and the nation. Cooley's Doctrine reinforces this by viewing local entities as organic expressions of popular will, not requiring explicit constitutional mention to affirm their autonomy.

The Founders were well aware of counties' evolution as foundational administrative and justice units, beginning with shires in **1634** in Virginia and expanding to counties/parishes by the mid-**1600's** across colonies. These served as seats for local governance, handling courts, records, and community affairs, forming the base layer of representative government. In this Cooley-aligned framework, counties embodied the people's sovereign right to self-organize, predating Dillon's Rule by almost 200 years, and aligning with the Founders' Anglo-American traditions where local units like counties were inherent to republicanism, not mere state creations.[18] Their role as building blocks is evident in how most states formed Senate and House districts around counties, ensuring geographic and local interests influenced state legislation.

Regional Variations in Local Governance Models

Regional differences in colonial practices further illustrate counties' integral yet adaptable role in popular sovereignty:

- **New England** (Massachusetts, Connecticut, New Hampshire, Rhode Island): Emphasized town-centered governance, with counties functioning as primarily administrative purposes for conveniences like courts, reflecting a direct, community-driven self-rule that the Founders like Adams praised as pure republicanism.
- **Mid-Atlantic** (New York, Pennsylvania, New Jersey, Delaware, Maryland): Counties served as core political units, managing elections and justice, embodying the layered sovereignty where locals checked state power.
- **Southern** (Virginia, North Carolina, South Carolina, Georgia): Counties (or parishes) were dominant, handling broad administration, aligning with Jefferson's ward system ideal where small republics (counties) fostered civic virtue.

These variations, rooted in colonia charter, demonstrate how popular sovereignty allowed flexible local forms without constitutional prescription, per Cooley's inherent rights view.

The silence of the use of the term "County" is not significant, due to general understandings of the time and since the focus is on the rights of Popular Sovereignty being inherent with 'the People". What further supports this is in how the ratification of the Constitution took place with representative votes, beginning with the counties.

Counties then appear to be the parents to the formation of good state governance, making the state the child, with the counties having the role as parents. Why does this matter, it ensures that "We the People" can protect the 'Popular Sovereignty' that the founding fathers envisioned.

Checks and Balances Rooted in Popular Sovereignty

The systems of checks and balances deliberately empower "We the People" as having the ultimate check on all government levels, with counties historically checking state policy through mechanisms like county-based state senates—pre-Reynolds v. Sims (**1964**), wherein many upper houses apportioned one senator per county or district, ensuring rural and local voices balanced population-heavy areas. This structure, aligned with the Founders' federalism, preserved popular sovereignty by preventing state dominance over locals, as Cooley advocated for inherent local checks to safeguard liberty. Though altered by one-person-one-vote rulings, this historical design underscores counties' parental role in nurturing good state governance, ensuring the people's inherent rights remain protected.

In summary, the Constitution's framework, by omitting explicit county mentions yet relying on their practical role in representation and ratification, affirms popular sovereignty as the "foundational truth" allowing layered government from counties to nation, in line with Cooley's Doctrine and the Founders' vision of self-governing republics.[19]

The States have a check on the federal body of government, as only limited enumerated powers were granted to the federal body. The People are to have a check on the State governments, through counties.

The Federal body is checked internally by each of the **3** branches of government having checks on each other and the Representative bodies of the House and Senate have unique representation that does not ensure a popular vote of democracy, but one of a representative vote, the House by population and the Senate by fixed geographies (the states). **The Framers' original design** — were meant to keep them in check forever, ***with the ultimate check***, an Article V Convention by the States. Again, something that has been lost upon the states.

This isn't metaphor. It's constitutional mechanics.

From **1787** until the mid-**20th** century, almost every new state entered the Union the same way: through an **Enabling Act** passed by Congress. As time moved on, it appears that Congress began modifying the admission process so that new states were not admitted on the exact same terms as the original **13** states, Enabling Acts began to put out new requirements.

Consider the process of ratification, wherein early processes involved representative and not popular votes. The founders knew all too well the risks of popular votes through democracies, hence they devised a true representative process of consensus building, utilizing a bicameral congress for consensus. Counties weren't afterthoughts; they were the sovereign building blocks. Yet states like Washington entered the union, with Congress stipulating that the vote for acceptance of the state constitution had to be by popular vote.

How did your state vote on their initial state constitution, by ***popular*** *or* ***representative*** *vote?*

How the Original 13 Colonies/States Gave Birth to the Model

While the original thirteen colonies didn't spring from counties — counties sprang from them. But even there, the pattern held: local jurisdictions (counties, parishes, townships) were the foundational units of representation.

When the states ratified the U.S. Constitution (**1787–1791**), they did it through county representative votes in convention. Either this has been an oversight in our education system, or a deliberate intent to undermine our early foundation. Either way the Truth is that the ratification was not centered on statewide popular votes, but through elected delegates from each county, aggregating a representative vote into state conventions. **Virginia's 1788** convention?[20] **168** delegates, representing each county or borough. **New York's**?[21] County caucuses decided the yea/nay state vote. Other counties and states did likewise, with delegates representing their communities.

This wasn't casual. The Upper Chamber or Senates in State legislatures, early on mirrored the federal structure: states were the fixed geographical basis within the U.S. Senate, just as counties were often the fixed geographical basis for representation within the state senate. Yes, it is true that some states have an unusually high number of counties, which also allowed for counties to be grouped together into senate districts. ***These districts are not to be adjusted with census updates, yet county lines are to remain fixed, and are not to be subject to gerrymandering.***

Consider that any urban state, has the right to increase their U.S. Senate representation, if Congress agrees, after the subject state petitions to be split. Kentucky successfully split from Virginia in **1792**, Maine from Massachusetts in **1820** and West Virginia from Virginia in **1863**. Proposals have been laid out for California and Florida to do the same, but these efforts have not succeeded yet.

If a county within a state is an urban county, they always have the right to follow the same pattern or form, by petitioning their state legislature to subdivide, which could then allocate the right for an additional state senate seat of representation as a new county is created. The reality, the state senate represents fixed geographies within a state, modeling itself after the U.S. Senate.

A great beauty of the U.S. Constitution is in the simplicity of its design, and yet the complexity by which it covers so much territory in how it lays out the modeled structure of governance at all levels of government. ***If we can just return to the Constitution, we will find answers to all our governing problems.***

Original State Senate Apportionment (1790)

The 13 original states State Senate's apportionment ~1790 at the time of Constitutional Ratification				
State	Constitution Year	Upper Chamber Name	Number of Senators (Initial/1780s)	Counties/Districts State Senate Notes
Delaware	1776	Legislative Council in 1790, the Senate in 1792	9 (3 per county)	3 counties; 3 senators each
Pennsylvania	1776 (unicameral until 1790)	Senate (1790)	The first senate was 18 members	1790 Senate districts were both multi and single county. No counties were split.
New Jersey	1776	Legislative Council	13 (1 per county)	13 counties
Georgia	1777 (unicameral until 1789)	Senate (1790, new Constitution takes effect.)	12 New counties were added after 1790's, adding more senate seats.	Unicameral initially, bicameral in 1789, Senate based on County representation
Connecticut	1776 (based on 1662 charter)	Council (Council of Assistants)	12	At-large or county-based
Massachusetts	1780	Senate	40	District-based--property/tax
Maryland	1776	Senate	15 (indirectly elected)	9 electors per shore (District) / county chose senators
South Carolina	1778	Senate	13–20 (variable)	Parish/district-based, later shifting to Counties with the 1895 Constitution, shifting senate representation to equal apportionment by county, regardless of population.
New Hampshire	1784	Senate	12–24 (variable early)	District-based
Virginia	1776	Senate	24	24 districts, (single-county or multi-county districts).
New York	1777	Senate	24	4 districts (multi-county, southern, middle, eastern, western); varying per district
North Carolina	1776	Senate	13 (1 per county)	Initially 1 per county (13 counties)
Rhode Island	1663 Royal Charter Constitution in 1843.	House of Magistrates In 1843 becomes the Senate	Started as a unicameral body in 1663, moving to bicameral in 1696. In 1790, *based on fixed geographies.*	The 1696 move was to an upper house (House of Magistrates). The change in 1843, moved to a senate with one senator per city.

Exhibit-5

The Senate apportionment was done by fixed boundaries, counties or districts associated by counties. In the case of Rhode Island, the move was eventually to the fixed boundaries of defined cities. South

Carolina even moved to county apportionment regardless of the population influence.

Sampling of County Influence on Process

Sampling of County Influence on Process
Ratification by Representation or Popular Vote

State	Year	Ratification method	Notes	Popular Vote
The 13 original states (ratifying the U.S. Constitution)	1787–1790	Specially elected state ratifying conventions (delegates chosen by counties or towns)	Convention-County	No
Ohio	1802–1803	Convention drafted → submitted to Congress only	Convention-County	No
Missouri	1820–1821	Convention adopted → sent to Congress after long fight over slavery clause	Convention-County	No
Kentucky (from Virginia)	1792	Virginia legislature consented; Kentucky convention adopted	Convention-County	No
Tennessee (from North	1796	Territorial-style convention adopted	Convention-County	No
Louisiana	1812	Convention adopted → sent to Congress	Convention-County	No
Indiana	1816	Convention adopted → sent to Congress	Convention-County	No
Mississippi	1817	Convention adopted → sent to Congress	Convention-County	No
Illinois	1818	Convention adopted → sent to Congress	Convention-County	No
Alabama	1819	Convention adopted → sent to Congress	Convention-County	No
Arkansas	1836	Convention adopted → sent to Congress	Convention-County	No
Michigan	1837	Convention adopted → sent to Congress	Convention-County	No
Rhode Island (*Revised state constitution, not admission*)	1842	First widespread use of popular referendum on a state constitution (the "Freemen's Constitution" was rejected, then *the 1843 one was approved by popular vote*)	Sparked the movement	No-Yes
Texas (annexation constitution)	1845	**Submitted to direct vote of the people** (approved 4,174 to 312, out of a population of 125,000+)	First admission-era use	Yes
Iowa	1846	First territorial admission that required a popular vote on the constitution (1844 draft rejected by voters; 1846 draft approved) 7,700+ votes cast for a population of 1000,000+	Popular vote	Yes
Wisconsin	1848	1846 draft rejected by popular vote; 1848 draft approved by popular vote	Popular vote	Yes
California	1849–50	Convention drafted → popular referendum (approved 1849) → sent to Congress	Popular vote	Yes
Minnesota	1858	Popular referendum required	Popular vote	Yes
Oregon	1859	Popular referendum required	Popular vote	Yes

Exhibit 6

Source: U.S. Statutes at Large; state constitutional histories.

Territories to States: The Enabling Act Recipe

Congress didn't just wave a wand for new states. Under Article IV, Section 3 (Admissions Clause), most of the **37** post-**1787** states required an **Enabling Act** — a congressional invitation that said, in effect:

> *"Territorial legislatures use your counties and draft your state constitution. We'll approve if it's republican in form and upholds both the Declaration of Independence and the U.S. Constitution."*

Take Washington Territory "WA" as an example. An intriguing example since the citizens approved two constitutions (**1877** & **1889**). The first state constitution was approved by the state before the Enabling Act was issued. Here is a brief summary:

<u>1853 </u>**Organic Act**[22]: Congress created the territory from Oregon lands, empowering **county-based legislatures.**

1878 Constitutional Convention[23]: The initial Washington state Constitution is rejected by Congress (Historian Dorothy Johansen speculates that Democrats were concerned over the admission of a Republican-leaning state.) The number of legislative districts would be **10** and never to exceed **20**. Yet by **2025**, WA has **49** Legislative Districts. *"The Senate shall consist of one third the number of members of the House of Representations."* An interesting observation as we move on.

1889 Enabling Act[24]: Passed on February 22;
> *"provided for the division of Dakota into two States and to enable the people of North Dakota, South Dakota, Montana and Washington to form constitutions and State governments and to be admitted into the Union **on an equal footing** with the original States…"*

The conventions were authorized to form constitutions and State governments, which were to be *"republican in form"* **and** *"not be repugnant to the Constitution of the United States and the principles of the Declaration of Independence."*

1889 Washington State Constitution

Finally, the *constitution was to be submitted to the people for ratification* by the first Tuesday in October. This last requirement was a clear violation of the "equal footing" doctrine. **The original States ratified the U.S. Constitution, by a representative vote and not by popular vote.**

Texas was the outlier (annexed as a republic in **1845**, since it had won its independence from Mexico in **1836**), but even there: delegates through conventions [25]drafted the **1836** Republic charter, establishing a bicameral legislature, and **1845** constitutions.

> *"The state is but a collection of counties, and the county the true unit of local self-government."*
>
> — Justice Stephen Field,
> California Supreme Court, **1860's**
> (echoing the federal model)

Why Counties Were "Sovereign" (Limited, But Real)

In America, individuals and Counties are not vassals, but should enjoy the benefits of *"popular sovereignty"*[26]. Yet we find that use of this terminology is avoided. The terms **"quasi-sovereign"** or **"little republics"**, may not have been written into early state constitutions, yet they were used in various capacities to describe government for the people. Thomas Jefferson in a letter to John Adams used the term *"little republics"* [27]to describe towns and counties as miniature self-governing units. *"Quasi-Sovereign"* was used by courts to describe the special standing of states in protecting their citizens. Examples of

County self-governance can be seen as:

- **Taxation authority:** collecting taxes for funding roads, schools and courts. Don't expect this to disappear.
- **Electing Sheriffs:** Sheriffs are the senior law enforcer within a county and a position that has existed for over 1,000 years in English Law. Yet there is a progressive movement to nullify the elected position of county sheriff in WA State, and perhaps in other states.
- **Forming Militias:** In colonial America, counties organized militias for defense. County militias have all but disappeared, in many states.
- **Local justice system:** County courts were the primary judicial authority, until the state supreme courts developed. As a result of the state bar associations, even county courts are impacted by the policies and politics of a state.
- **Securing agreements** with neighboring counties.

Once again, shouldn't counties be afforded the same privilege, through Popular Sovereignty, to ensure the protection of the interests of "We the People?

Dillon's Rule (1868) moved to centralize power to states, by limiting the decision making by counties. Yet, Home-Rule counties are led to believe that they have autonomy in their decision making. In the end, under Dillon's Rule, Counties, even Home-Rule counties, are treated more like vassals and subject to State controls. Dillion's Rule is a pseudo argument for legal interpretation that has no basis in what the founding fathers intended. The entirety of the argument started out as a legal theory nearly **100** years after the Constitution was signed and has now been moved into legal process with standing, or so we are told.

What has been lost is the counterbalance to Dillon's Rule, is the 'Cooley Doctrine'.

As identified in "Are local government Mere Creatures of the States?" The authors Paul R. DeHart and Ronald J. Oakerson state:

"Cooley's account of local authority, by contrast, is grounded in the popular-sovereignty model advanced by the founders. According to this view, the highest political authority in a regime remains the people. The people, not the state, possess the authority to create and dissolve governments. And under a republican regime, local self-government is a fundamental right of the people. It follows that, in the United States, local authority grounds state action, rather than the reverse. Local Government therefore cannot, as a matter of principle, depend on the exercise of state authority".

> "Republican form also depends on federal form, understood broadly to apply to the relations among all levels of government — national, state, and local. …
> To subject local communities to the political whims of state governors on this suspect basis poses a manifest danger to the republic."
> **—Paul R. DeHart, Ronald J. Oakerson**

Later in the same article the authors stated "Historically, as Lutz has argued, the authority of local officials was legitimized by community covenants in an expression of **popular sovereignty**."[28]

The Guarantee Clause (Art. IV, §4) **wasn't optional:** it bound Congress to reject any state constitution that deviated from the

"Republican Form of Government" which was to be Representative. By example, the model we find is the federal bicameral model, wherein the House is apportioned by population and the Senate by fixed geographies. (Yes, it is true that Nebraska intentionally moved from a bicameral to a unicameral state government, but this was done on their own, and not by any judicial gerrymandering of SCOTUS.)

All of this was fine, until the **20th** century, when "progress" meant efficiency — and efficiency meant erasing rural voices. The move to return to full democracy continued (Pre-U.S. Constitution).

That erosion starts in the next chapter. But remember that counties didn't just build the states. They were meant to bridle them, the same as states are meant to bridle the federal body of government.

Action Item:
- Map your state's original senate districts (**pre-1964**).
- How many were modeled on the use of fixed geographies, or the use of counties?
- Use this information to rally your commissioners: "This is what the Framers ordered."
- Then compare with your neighboring states.

Chapter 3

The Connecticut Compromise, at the State Level:

The Guarantee of a Republican (representative) form of government for states.

"A republican form is 'a government which derives all its powers directly or indirectly from the great body of the people'…"
— **James Madison**, Federalist No. 10

The Connecticut Compromise (**1787**) didn't just save the federal convention. It became the unbreakable template for every state legislature. Representation by population in the House, using fixed geographies in the Senate. No exceptions.

Why? Because without it, democracy devours republics. And the Framers knew republics die when cities steamroll the countryside. **Aristotle** states: *"Republics decline into democracies and democracies degenerate into despotisms."*[29]

The Deadlock That Almost Killed the Union

(**The Great Compromise**)[30] Philadelphia, summer **1787**. The Virginia Plan (big states, population-based everything) clashed with the New Jersey Plan (small states, equal votes). Tempers flared. Benjamin Franklin prayed for wisdom. Then Roger Sherman and Oliver Ellsworth dropped the bomb:

- **House**: Proportional to population (protects the "people").
- **Senate**: Originally designed to represent the interests of the state legislature, this was also to ensure that the framers

demand for equal representation for each state (protecting the "communities" — geography, land, resources, and the minority interests of more rural states).

It passed **5–4–1** (with one abstention). Madison called it "the engine of the Constitution." But here's the key no one teaches: the Framers did not explicitly demand that states mirror this, however it was such a great idea that all states eventually got onboard. ***The Guarantee Clause wasn't fluff — it was a core principle of Truth.***

From Madison's Notes (Constitutional Convention, July 1787):
"Mr. Madison considered the popular election of one branch of the national legislature as essential to every plan of free Govt… In the other branch, the States shd. be represented… not according to their sizes, but as equal political bodies."

Translation: States aren't mini-democracies. They're mini-republics, with counties as the "states" in that equation.

State Ratification: Counties as the Ratifiers
Proof? Look at ratification.
- **Pennsylvania (1787):** County meetings elected delegates; Antifederalists from rural counties nearly tanked it.
- **Massachusetts (1788):** County conventions demanded the Bill of Rights as price for a yes vote.
- **North Carolina (1789):** 5 months of county debates; rural counties flipped the vote.

By **1791**, all thirteen had bicameral legislatures. Eleven with county-based senates. The two which had been unicameral holdouts (Pennsylvania, Georgia) adapted quickly to bicameral legislatures.

Timeline Sidebar: The Federal Analogy Spreads (1787–1800)
- **1787**: Connecticut Compromise locks federal model.
- **1788**: Virginia ratifies via county vote (89–79).
- **1791**: Vermont statehood, with unicameral legislature
- **1800**: **16** states, **15** of which were bicameral. Vermont was the holdout, till **1836.**

Federalist Papers: The Blueprint for States

Hamilton, Madison, Jay didn't hold back, they clarified from what they could anticipate.

Federalist No 2 (Jay): *"This country and this people … made for each other… as if by the design of Providence, that an inheritance so proper and convenient for a band of brethren, united to each other by the strongest ties… With equal pleasure I have as often taken notice that Providence has been pleased to give this one connected country to one united people…"* Consider how this also applies to the counties in being united by boundaries within a state, and hopefully united in purpose.

Federalist No. 17 (Hamilton): *"The administration of criminal and civil justice … The administration of private justice between the citizens of the same State, the supervision of agriculture and similar concerns of a similar nature, all those things, in short, which are proper to be provided for by local legislation, can never be desirable cares of a general jurisdiction."* Again, apply this modeled thinking to the contiguous relationship of counties within a state.

Federalist No. 28 (Hamilton): Describes how if the federal government becomes tyrannical, resistance will begin at the most local level and work upward. That the people's right to self defense supersedes the government, drawing the comparison that under the weak Articles of Confederation, that individual states could become tyrannical without a federal check. This is exactly why the counties should have the ability to adapt the use of a Convention of Counties, to restore representative balance within the state senate, seeing how SCOTUS overreached and unfairly removed a representative tool for governance.

Federalist No. 39 (Madison): Republican form means *"deriving all its powers directly or indirectly from the great body of the people… not from an inconsiderable proportion or a favored class of it…"* The analysis by Madison on the foundation, sources of power, extent of powers, mode of exercise and structure of government; then consider *"Republican Form of Government"*, all support the idea that counties are the building block to representative government within states.

> **Consider** how homes and families are the building blocks to localized government; then starting with the counties as we then move forward into the construction of states and a nation. The form is key.

Federalist No. 46 (Madison): Citizens will have stronger attachment to state and local government as he describes the impact of county offices and these offices will be in constant communication with the people, as they are *"vigilant guardians of their rights"*. Federal tyranny should not be a concern, as local (county) and state office holders will ensure a protection of the interests of the people. Madison was clear about what he saw, as a constitution that ensured localized engagement and controls.

Federalist No. 62 (Madison): *"The fabric of American empire ought to rest on the solid basis of the consent of the people… A government ill executed, however good, is ruinous to the people."* But for states: *"The senate is to represent the states as political bodies."* Clearly showing how the structure of the (U.S.) Senate with its equal representation of the states, regardless of population and longer six-year terms with staggered elections was to be modeled.

Once again "Form" is critical in understanding how state governments emulated the model provided for by the states at the federal level of government creation. Not only did states adapt to the bicameral system, they also emulated the terms for service within the state senates as state senates are normally for a longer term than state house seats and as a result are staggered into tiers of senate classes, with one class being elected in odd years and the other being elected in even years, or for periods offset from state house seats. The U.S. Senate is seated in three tiers or classes, elected in even numbered years.

Was this a coincidence, or by design in "form"?

Why It Mattered: Protecting the Minority

Urban areas grow. Rural ones, not as fast. Without fixed senate seats, cities dictate. The Framers saw it in England, with rotting boroughs. They weren't letting it happen here.

In Washington State, the **1889** constitution echoed this: Senate districts = counties. Until Reynolds gutted it.

The Great Compromise wasn't compromise. It was genius. And it worked — until five justices in **1964** decided they knew better.

Action Item: Host a "Federal Analogy Night" at your county courthouse.

- Should we apply the same standards for 'form of government' to the States, as we have in Congress?
- Should our state senate be apportioned equally by county?
- Consider if you like how a car drives. If you were to order the same car for your pleasure, would you want it to be changed without your permission?

Chapter 4

The Judicial Coup of 1962–1964

Baker, Gray, Wesberry, and Reynolds in Plain English

"These decisions… are nothing less than an exercise of the amending power by this Court."

— Justice John Marshall Harlan II,
Dissent in Reynolds v. Sims (**1964**)

**Four cases. One decade.
Total war on the republican form.**

But the Warren Court didn't open with a frontal assault. It started with a **distraction** — one that divided the country, inflamed the culture, and kept rural America looking the wrong way while the real coup unfolded.

Opening Salvo: Engel v. Vitale (June 25, 1962) – The Distraction

Focus on official prayers within public schools.

A 22-word, non-denominational prayer in New York public schools:

"Almighty God, we acknowledge our dependence upon Thee, and we beg Thy blessings upon us, our parents, our teachers and our country."

The Court struck it down 6–1. No coercion. No establishment. Just a voluntary prayer. Students could remain silent or leave the room.

49

The ruling came to be applied to neutral and even non-compulsory prayers. People became confused and distracted as they worked to understand the full impact.

Justice Hugo Black wrote: *"It is no part of the business of government to compose official prayers."*

Rural America erupted. Congress introduced over 200 constitutional amendments to restore school prayer within the next two years. Petitions flooded county courthouses. Ministers preached about it from pulpits. This was the **Perfect distraction.**

While the nation waited on the decision in the fight over God in classrooms, the Court decided **Baker v. Carr** — the case that would eventually let federal judges redraw every state senate in America.

Step 2: Baker v. Carr (March 26, 1962) – The Breach

Focus: Can federal courts judicially review state reapportionment?

Tennessee hadn't redrawn districts since **1901**. Urban Atlanta boomed; rural counties withered. Voters sued: unequal representation!

Warren's Court ruled **6–2**: Justiciable. Federal courts can now police state legislative maps.

Justice Frankfurter (dissent): "This Court has no business entering the political thicket… The Guarantee Clause is for Congress, not us."

Too late. The door was open.

Step 3: Gray v. Sanders (1963) – The Escalation

Focus: on Statewide elections, e.g., Governor, U.S. Senator.

The case was focused on primary elections, for statewide offices, by apportioning votes based on county populations. While SCOTUS decided for political equality, in primary elections, the decision would become more impactful in a year for all elections.

For now, the decision landed in favor of the urban center of Fulton County.

Gray: Georgia's county-unit system for statewide elections?

Dead, rural counties would be impacted negatively. The concept now of "One person, one vote", became a principle and edged into law for everything.

Step 4: Wesberry v. Sanders (1964) – The Congressional Hook

Focus: on U.S. House seats

Congressional districts must be equal population. Fair — but the Court would end up using this as a precedent for state legislatures.

While congressional House seats had always been apportioned to a state based on population, the size of the congressional district did not always follow. For example, the 5th District in Georgia (Atlanta) had a population of over 800,000, some of the more rural districts had as few as 300,000 residents. Meaning that a rural vote in Georgia could have a value of **2-3x** more value than that of Atlanta residents. Mind you, this was for the U.S. House seats. Hence the gerrymandering of U.S. House seats now became a tool for greater abuse.

Step 5: Reynolds v. Sims (1964) – The Kill Shot

Focus: One person one vote, for both State Senate and House

Alabama's Senate: county based. House: population. Classic federal analogy.

Warren: Nope. Both houses must be population-based. "Legislators represent people, not trees or acres."

Overnight: 41 states' senates gutted.

Harlan's Dissent:

"The Equal Protection Clause was never intended to inhibit the States in choosing any democratic method they pleased for the apportionment of their legislatures… This is shown by the language of the Fourteenth Amendment… and by the political practices of the States at the time."

Harlan shredded it: The 14th Amendment's framers deliberately left state apportionment to states (see §2, which penalizes vote denial but doesn't mandate equality). Ratification history? States kept unequal senates. Post-14th amendments (19th, 24th)? They assume states set rules.

He lost 8–1.

The Almost-Save: Dirksen's Amendment

Illinois Senator Everett Dirksen (R) fought back. S.J. Res. 2 (**1965**): Allow states to keep geo-based senates if voters approve.

Passed Senate **65–30**. Fell short of **2/3** in House. Cities lobbied hard.

Why the Engel Distraction Matters

- **Divided the resistance:** Rural counties were busy passing resolutions defending school prayer while their political power was being erased.
- **Softened the ground:** *If the Court could ban voluntary prayer, who would believe it couldn't redraw maps?*
- **Cultural wedge:** Pitted religious conservatives against urban secularists — exactly the divide that would later let urban centers (cities) dominate state legislatures.

The Warren Court played 4D chess. We were playing checkers.

Another Rabbit Hole, Tribal Nations (Sovereign or not)

A generalized search will show that Native American tribes, or Tribal Nations, are sovereign nations. But then again, are they?

A quick search asking about Tribal nations being recognized as being sovereign nations will probably provide an answer along the lines of "*Tribal nations are recognized as sovereign entities within the United States, possessing the inherent authority to govern themselves.*

Tribes have the right to self-determination and can exercise their powers independently, although they may face restrictions from the federal government."

What may have been a pivot point in the evolution of tribal governments, requires a look at the Indian Reorganization Act of 1934[31].

Two key provisions of the Act are Sections 16 and 17:

Section 16 – Tribal Constitutions and Bylaws

Any Indian tribe, or tribes, residing on the same reservation, shall have the right to organize for its common welfare, and *may adopt an appropriate constitution and bylaws*, which shall become effective *when ratified by a majority vote of the adult members of the tribe*, or of the adult Indians residing on such reservation, as the case may be, at a special election authorized and called by the Secretary of the Interior under such rules and regulations as he may prescribe. Such constitution and bylaws, when ratified as aforesaid and approved by the Secretary of the Interior, *shall be revocable by an election similarly called and conducted*. Every such constitution shall provide that *the tribe shall have power to regulate its internal and social relations and to control its property, and may make any other provisions not inconsistent with the laws of the United States*.

Section 17 – Tribal Corporations (Companion provision allowing tribes to charter corporations for economic development)

The Secretary of the Interior may, *upon petition by at least one-third of the adult Indians*, issue a charter of incorporation to such tribe: Provided, that such charter *shall not become operative until ratified at a special election by a majority vote of the adult Indians* living on the reservation. Such charter may convey to the incorporated tribe the power to purchase, take by gift, or bequest, or otherwise, own, hold, manage, operate, and dispose of property of every description, real and personal...

Consider that this was done in **1934**, well after the Statehood of **48** States, and more than **100** years after the creation of the Bureau of Indian Affairs "BIA" (**1824**). Apparently, the Secretary of the Interior has the authority to grant approval for Constitutional creation and approval. Yet it also states that "*Every such constitution shall provide*" that the tribe shall have power to regulate its internal and social relations and to control its property and **may make any other provisions not inconsistent with the laws of the United States**. On the surface this is fine, until you realize that We the People never delegated this power to the Secretary of the Interior. Only Congress has the right to enter into Treaties and agreements with foreign nations. *The U.S. Constitution is also clear about the idea that States cannot be created within the borders of states.* ***Why then would we allow for a foreign nation to be created within a state?***

How about the idea that Congress is saying that within this Act, with as simple as **1/3** of the adults signing a petition, that a Charter can be issued. This same Charter would then be ratified when approved by a majority vote of the people. Once again, we see the early movement from Representative votes to Popular votes, and a vote where a simple majority can prevail. The second dynamic is that of how the Tribal Nation can enact and do what they want, yet they are beholden to the Secretary of the Interior. ***So, are they to be a sovereign nation, or do they enjoy a level of popular sovereignty?***

Why do Tribal Nations enjoy greater representation within government process over that of counties?

If most tribes had no written constitutions prior to **1934**, then governance must have been subject to the BIA, as overseen by the Secretary of the Interior. Yet the U.S. Constitution states in Article 1, Section 8, Clause 3 *"The Congress shall have Power… To regulate Commerce with foreign Nations, and among the several States, and with the Indian Tribes…"*. So, Congress is the ultimate authority in relation to Tribal issues. The only other area where there is a reference is in Article 1, Section 2 Clause 3, *"Representatives and direct Taxes shall be apportioned among the several States… excluding Indians not taxed…"*

The simple meaning here, *"Indians not taxed"* meant tribal members living under tribal jurisdiction (on reservations) were not counted for congressional seats or taxes. Yet by the **14**[th] Amendment (**1868**) and later in the Indian Citizenship Act **1924**, All Native Americans are now full citizens and counted in the U.S. Census every **10** years.

So how does this relate, **The U.S. Constitution**:
> ***does not*** declare Tribal Nation's sovereignty,
> ***does not*** declare the creation of Reservations,
> ***does not*** identify Treaties, Citizenship or even the right
> to unique land ownership, for Tribal nations?

The Constitution does treat Indian tribes as distinct political entities—not states, not foreign nations, but "domestic dependent nations" as described by Chief Justice John Marshall in **1831**, resembling that of a "ward to its guardian".

Counties, while not mentioned explicitly within the Constitution, were utilized in the ratification process of the U.S. Constitution, through this process of representative government. Tribal nations had no role to play in Constitutional ratification, yet tribal nations today have greater rights and powers than our individual counties.

Would it make a difference if Counties were to write their own constitutions, if they were congruent with the U.S. Constitution?

Is this what is needed to ensure a qualifier for Popular Sovereignty?

Attorneys may suggest that the laws created, and rulings rendered by the courts, are what dictate how we are to lead our lives. If so, then we have ***a judicial form of government.*** But we don't, we have a **Constitutional, representative government** that is '***Republican in Form***'.

The only true sovereign entity as laid out in our Declaration of Independence, the U.S. Constitution and the Bill of Rights, are "We the People". The people are the ultimate sovereign authority. Building off of that, counties should be the next layer of government, followed by the states and then the nation.

What appears to be the birth of a nation in **1776**, was really the iteration of a process wherein The People, finally recognized that they were indeed Sons and Daughters of a living God, and that this God of Nature is in control of all things. We inherit all these rights from God, and in turn have been granted the right by God to manage these rights as we exercise self-governance. Our homes, communities, towns, counties all existed before our States or Nation. The **13** original states came to learn and understand how critical balance was within a representative form of government. They in turn agreed to and implemented this within the federal body of governance. So, what was first, The People, then the Counties, then the States and finally the Federal government.

People → Counties → States →Federal

Our representative state government, needs to include state senates, following the model of our U.S. Senate, with equal apportionment by fixed county (parish) districts.

The Proof in the Poison Fruit: Post-Reynolds:
- **Gun laws pass** within urban supermajorities (rural no-vote).
- **Taxes skyrocket** (cities don't feel property tax pain).
- **Borders ignored** (sanctuary cities dictate).
- **Bureaucratic Regulations** accelerate

By **1950** states had drifted through progressive policies, then Reynolds finished the job: **with no state being able to guarantee to their counties representation in their state senate, modeling the U.S. Senate.**

Action Item:
Step 1, Become informed and expand a conversation.

Part II

The Theft

County	Type	
Adams Columbia Ferry Garfield Jefferson Klickitat Lincoln Okanogan Pend Oreille Skamania Stevens Wahkiakum	**Frontier-1** <u>No</u> dedicated Senate Seats	
Asotin Chelan Clallam Douglas Grant Grays Harbor Kittitas Lewis Pacific Whitman	**Frontier-2** <u>No</u> dedicated Senate Seats	
Franklin Island Mason San Juan Skagit Walla Walla Yakima	**Rural** <u>No</u> dedicated Senate Seats	
Benton *Clark (2)* Cowlitz ***King (13)*** Kitsap (1) ***Pierce (4)*** ***Snohomish (3)*** *Spokane (3)* Thurston (1) Whatcom (1)	*(Urban Counties)* Non-Rural **Dedicated Senate** districts shown in (#)	**Note:** 31 Counties out of 39, have no dedicated State Senate Seats. Yet King, Pierce & Snohomish influence 28 Senate seats out of 49, for <u>**57% Influence.**</u>

Exhibit 8

Chapter 5

The Fruits of the Coup

How "One Person, One Vote" Delivered Urban Tyranny

"When the legislature is corrupted, the people are undone."
— John Adams

Reynolds v. Sims didn't just redraw maps. It **rewrote reality.**

Gerrymandering, which was introduced in **1812**, by the governor of Massachusetts, became a way to manipulate political power. If this were a game, it was one which the founding fathers did not envision, one which now was going to change course of a representative government process.

In **1964**, rural counties lost their permanent voice in state government, with gerrymandering taking on a new role, to ensure that state governments could now be managed by pure majority control of popular urban votes. In **2025**, we're living with the consequences.

This chapter is the **damage report**, using as an example, the impact on Washington State. Ask yourself, how does your state compare?

Consider that through State and Federal designations, Counties are classified as Frontier 1, Frontier 2, Rural and Non-Rural (Urban). Yet due to Gerrymandering, the Legislative Districts often consider the County boundaries to be irrelevant.

The problem becomes more pronounced as you move into the Non-rural or Urban centers. At this point the full damage occurs as Urban centers can now take advantage of their rural neighbors as they leverage the benefit of population against the natural resources.

Note that none of the Frontier 1 or 2, as well as the Rural counties within Washington State, enjoy any dedicated Senate seats to their county. While within the non-rural category, all but two have dedicated state senate seats.

- **King County** has **13 dedicated Senators**
- **Pierce** has **4**
- **Snohomish** has **3**
- **Spokane** has **3**
- **Clark** has **2**
- **Kitsap**, **Thurston** and **Whatcom** each have **1**
- **Benton** and **Cowlitz** each **have ZERO dedicated Senators** (*along with 29 other counties*.)

*Simply, **31** out of **39** counties*
have <u>NO Dedicated</u> Senate Representation.

3 Counties directly influence **57%** of the Senate and House seats, voted by the same people. The only difference is in the time that they serve, House members for **2** years, Senators for **4** years.

Exhibit 9

The diversity of natural resources is significant by county. Forests are abundant in the mountain areas and along the coastline. Coastal areas are abundant in shipping and marine life. The interior of the state is fed by the Columbia River, and with the arid climate is ideally suited for farming. The eastern region bumps up against the Rocky Mountains with an abundance of minerals.

Washington State—Münchausen by Olympia in Full Bloom

Crisis	Urban Vote (King, Pierce & Snohomish Counties)	Rural Reality	Likely Senate Veto power Pre-1964
Transgender Youth Laws SB-5599 2023	21% of Rural votes were Yea 75% of Rural votes were Nea	Parents stripped of custody if they refuse "gender-affirming care"	Yes
Sanctuary State-Keep Washington Working Act SB-5497 2019	30% of Rural votes were Yea 75% of Rural votes were Nea	ICE detainers ignored; fentanyl pours in	Yes
Carbon Tax / Gas Ban (2021–2024)	71 % yes	Rural gas prices +$1.50/gal; heating costs triple	Yes
Wildfire Mismanagement	68 % yes for "climate emergency"	2.7 million acres burned 2020–2025; forest funds diverted	Yes

Exhibit 10

King County (Seattle): **2.2** million people, **29%** of state population, **3%** of the land area, yet they control **13** (**27%**) of the State senate seats, outright, in a post-Reynolds SCOTUS decision.

The other **38** counties: **97** % of land, **71** % of people, with **31** of the **39** counties having no dedicated senate voice, of at least a single state senator dedicated to representing their interests.

This is occupation.

Examples of how a lack of a voice impacts policy:

SB-5599, The Gender Affirming Bill, 2023

This bill created enough awareness amongst the population that an Initiative was created, signed by the people and passed into law by the Legislature. Shortly thereafter the Executive branch leaders and Legislature, took steps to nullify the law by stating that the education system would not enforce the law, which was supported directly by The People.

SB-5599, The Gender Affirming Care Bill (any age) 2023					
Rural/Urban	LD	Yea's	Rural/Urban	LD	Nea's
Urban	1	Yea	Urban	2	NO
Urban	3	Yea	Urban	4	NO
Urban	5	Yea	Rural	6	NO
Urban	11	Yea	Rural	7	NO
Urban	21	Yea	Rural	8	NO
Rural	22	Yea	Rural	9	NO
Rural	23	Yea	Rural	10	NO
Rural	24	Yea	Urban	12	NO
Urban	26	Yea	Rural	13	NO
Urban	27	Yea	Rural	14	NO
Urban	28	Yea	Rural	15	NO
Urban	29	Yea	Rural	16	NO
Urban	30	Yea	Rural	17	NO
Urban	32	Yea	Rural	18	NO
Urban	33	Yea	Rural	19	NO
Urban	34	Yea	Rural	20	NO
Urban	36	Yea	Urban	25	NO
Urban	37	Yea	Rural	31	NO
Urban	38	Yea	Rural	35	NO
Rural	40	Yea	Urban	39	NO
Urban	41	Yea	Subtotal		20
Rural	42	Yea	75% of No votes were Rural		
Urban	43	Yea			
Urban	44	Yea			
Urban	45	Yea			
Urban	46	Yea			
Urban	47	Yea			
Urban	48	Yea			
Rural	49	Yea			
Subtotal		29			
21% of Yea votes were Rural					

Exhibit 11

SB-5497, the Immigrants in Workplace, 2019

"Keep Washington Working Act" was passed with well ahead of the immigration push of 2020 to 2024. The reality, this was designed to make Washington a sanctuary state for immigration.

By **2025**, the bill was being weaponized to restrict county sheriffs from working with ICE, to remove illegal immigrants.

Once again, the Rural voices are being outnumbered by the urban centers. Mind you, the Rural voices represent a number of the migrant workers and seasonal workers. They want to Keep Washington Working, yet they want to do it responsibly.

Next, we will find that well ahead of **2021**, the voters of Washington had rejected ballot measures like **Initiative 732 (2016)** "A revenue-neutral carbon tax on fossil fuels" and **Initiative 1631 (2018)** "A Carbon emissions fee" to fund clean energy.

SB-5497, 2019 Immigrants in the workplace or "Keep Washington Working Act"					
Rural/ Urban	LD	Yea's	Rural/ Urban	LD	Nea's
Urban	1	Yea	Urban	2	No
Urban	3	Yea	Urban	4	No
Urban	5	Yea	Rural	6	No
Urban	11	Yea	Rural	7	No
Rural	13	Yea	Rural	8	No
Rural	14	Yea	Rural	9	No
Rural	16	Yea	Rural	10	No
Rural	19	Yea	Urban	12	No
Urban	21	Yea	Rural	15	No
Rural	22	Yea	Rural	18	No
Rural	23	Yea	Rural	20	No
Rural	24	Yea	Rural	25	No
Urban	26	Yea	Rural	28	No
Urban	27	Yea	Rural	31	No
Urban	30	Yea	Urban	39	No
Urban	32	Yea	Rural	42	No
Urban	33	Yea	75% of No's were Rural		
Urban	34	Yea			
Urban	36	Yea			
Urban	37	Yea			
Urban	38	Yea			
Rural	40	Yea			
Urban	41	Yea			
Urban	43	Yea			
Urban	44	Yea			
Urban	45	Yea			
Urban	46	Yea			
Urban	47	Yea			
Urban	48	Yea			
Rural	49	Yea			
30% of Rural votes are Yea					

Exhibit 12

The Climate Commitment Act of 2021

SB-5126, passed with only **30%** of the Rural counties voting Yea and **82%** of the Rural counties voting no.

SB-5126, 2021 The Climate Commitment act (Carbon Tax Credit)					
Rural/ Urban	LD	Yea's	Rural/ Urban	LD	Nea's
Urban	1	Yea	Rural	20	No
Urban	3	Yea	Rural	8	No
Urban	5	Yea	Rural	16	No
Urban	11	Yea	Rural	42	No
Urban	21	Yea	Rural	31	No
Urban	22	Yea	Rural	25	No
Rural	23	Yea	Urban	12	No
Urban	26	Yea	Rural	6	No
Urban	27	Yea	Rural	15	No
Urban	28	Yea	Rural	14	No
Urban	29	Yea	Rural	40	No
Urban	30	Yea	Urban	2	No
Urban	32	Yea	Rural	10	No
Urban	33	Yea	Urban	4	No
Urban	34	Yea	Rural	18	No
Rural	35	Yea	Rural	9	No
Urban	36	Yea	Rural	7	No
Urban	37	Yea	Rural	24	No
Urban	38	Yea	Urban	39	No
Urban	41	Yea	Rural	13	No
Urban	43	Yea	Rural	17	No
Urban	44	Yea	Rural	19	No
Urban	45	Yea	82% of Rural votes were NO		
Urban	46	Yea			
Urban	47	Yea			
Urban	48	Yea			
Rural	49	Yea			
30% of Rural votes were Yea					

Exhibit 13

Like all environmental laws, they are born with good intentions, and then they seem to take on a life of their own. Enacted in **2021**, the purpose was to cap and reduce greenhouse emissions from the state's largest polluters.

By **2024** the citizens of Washington State saw fit to sign Initiative-**2117**, to take the matter to the people on a vote. State leaders then commandeered resources to launch a campaign to persuade a vote that favored maintaining the Carbon Tax program. Did the people really want the highest gas prices in the nation? **As gas prices averaged $3.04/gal in November 2025, WA maintained the position of 3rd highest in the nation at $4.19/gal, just behind CA at $4.59 and HI at $4.44/gal.**[32]

In the end, we are finding a more bloated bureaucracy with funding going into areas having no relation to environment.[33] As $4 billion CO2 taxes are collected in **2** years (starting **2023**), consider where the money is going.

Wildfire Management and insanity

As the new Lands Commissioner in WA, (**2025**) concludes his first year in office, we find that the best that can be offered up, give us more money and maybe we can manage the problem. Forest fires have existed throughout history. Research will show that in the **1990's** WA experienced about **86,000** acres of forest per year burned, as compared to an average of **280,000** acres per year from **2000** to **2020**.

As for harvesting of timber, timber was harvested at a rate of about **5** billion board feet "BBF" annually, prior to **1990**. During the **90's** the harvest fell to about **4.5** BBF and in recent years to about **2.7** BBF. The Northwest Forest Plan, brought on by the Endangered Species Act, slashed much of the harvesting. Out of this harvest, about **25%** of the production is shipped overseas in the form of raw logs. In the process, cutting out the counties from being able to process the lumber.

The Homeless Industrial Complex

Of all programs this has been built from a never-ending appetite for raising taxes and spending money on a problem that is never Auditable, and which is centered to a large extent in the urban cores. Nearly a billion dollars per year, and the problem grows. [34] One of the wildest programs to be created is **the Housing Trust Fund,** wherein first-time disadvantage home buyers can receive up to **$150,000** in a forgivable loan, at zero percent interest. The point of even mentioning this, is that the rural counties within the state have little to no voice in the process. With a state senate apportioned by county, the opportunity would then exist to have a voice in managing the problem and solution.

National Poison Fruits (2020–2025)

- **Gun Control:** By **2023** at least **20** states passed red-flag laws in a post-Reynolds world. Rural sheriffs in WA State began to take a stand in **2019** as the popular vote in the State voted yes to tough new gun laws, setting the stage for **13** county sheriffs declaring a refusal to enforce.[35]
  - WA Rural Sheriffs, insights and opportunity.[36]
  - **Sheriff Mack** & Peaceful, Constitutional Solutions[37]
  - **Special note**: *as this book is going to print, the Sheriff of Pierce County, Keith Swank, is receiving national attention, as the State wants to now have the ability to decertify locally elected county sheriffs.* **What is next?**
- **Sanctuary Support** (Immigration): Coming onto the scene in the late **1970's** (Post Reynolds decision) the number of Sanctuary states, cities or counties has expanded to over **564** by **2018** and **1,003 by 2025**.[38] The waters were tested as major cities like San Francisco and New York City accepted the premise that they could support such policies. If ever there could be a policy that could be balanced with a

Representative voice from the counties, through their state senate, this would be one.

- **Tax Increases**: Nationally many states are reconsidering how they manage the taxation of single-family residences. Seniors are fearful that they do not own their home and are in fact just a tenant of the state, paying a rent in the form of a tax. Consider then the issue of Property Taxes in WA State. The Constitution allows for Real Estate to be taxed for the purpose of 1) public purposes and 2) for the support of the common schools,[39] (Article VII, §1 of State Constitution). Has the state gone too far?

  > Consider that when **97**% of the land area is held by **38** out of **39** counties, shouldn't the principle of "Taxation without representation", be applied to the voice of counties, having an equal voice in their state senate? This was a key reason for fighting for independence as a country. Then ask yourself, how is the taxing structure within your state impacted by urban centers?

  > Better yet, if the state inherited land when they became a state, for the benefit of schools and education, then why are property taxes so high?

- **School Boards:** CRT, gender ideology, mask mandates — all urban supermajority wins. Yet nothing is closer to home than the policies we allow to be supported within our schools, as we teach and train for the future of our communities.

The Warren Supreme Court further opened the door in **1962** as they decided with Engle v. Vitale, that state-sponsored prayer in public schools violated the Establishment Clause in the Constitution. This expanded the road to Judicially legislating from the bench. What followed was a decision in **1971** in Lemon v. Kurtzman that was finally unraveled in the **2022** decision of Kennedy v. Bremerton School District (a WA School District), allowing for a coach's personal prayer at a school event.

So, consider that the simple issue of prayer in schools has taken 60 years to be clarified. All of this was on the heels of the loss of representation by our counties in our state senates, wherein gerrymandered legislative districts could control through there urban centers. *Do we have 60 years to reverse the ideologies that come with CRT, gender ideology, mask mandates and whatever else may be thrown our way?*

The Human Cost
- **Adams County Sheriff Dale Wagner (2025)**: Sued by the AG for honoring ICE detainers.
- **Water rights**, an entire book can be written on the human cost of Water Rights. Yet we can rest assured that the rural counties understand best how to manage the use of water in the production of crops so that the urban centers can enjoy both the water and production that comes from good agriculture.
- **Federal Courts split on question of "Biological-Sex-Based Access Rule for School Restrooms (2024)"[40]**: Why does it seem we have moved our debates to the courts? Laws are

created by and for "We the People". As a nation we created our legislative body before we implemented our judicial branch of government. Restore the voice of Counties, back into the State Senate, thus ensuring a bicameral legislative process and yes you will have debate, maybe even compromise, as the urban and rural voices find harmony.

"[T]here is no practice... which tends to renovate the constitution, than a temporary retirement to the country..."
—John Sinclair,
The Code of Health and Longevity, c.**1815**

"Kings don't beg, they decree. They have only one destiny and that's to reign. God has made you king. Reign and rule, refuse to beg!"
—Chris Oyakhilome

While history will show a migration from the Rural to the Urban, due to advances in technology, the industrial revolution and so forth, ***there now seems to be a renewal in the return to and repopulating of our countryside.***[41]

Support for Convention of Counties

We, your constituents of ___________________________ County hereby notify you of our support for the calling of a "Convention of Counties", a concept that is modeled after an **Article 5, Convention of States.**

By our signature below, we are asking you to support this "Convention of Counties" to reapportion the Washington **State Senate to have equal representation from all 39 counties.**

Further, we support the election of the Senator upon ratification of agreement by 30 of the counties. **This office of State Senator is to represent the interests of the ENTIRE county.**

We support this Convention being called as soon as possible, so that we can have the representation as guaranteed in the U.S. Constitution.

Signature (As on voter registration)	Print Name	Address where you are registered	City	ZIP Code
Matt Hawkins	Matt Hawkins	200 S. Washington	Any	00000
2				
3				
4				
5				
6				
7				
8				
9				
10				
11				
12				
13				
14				
15				
16				
17				
18				
19				
20				

ConventionOfCounties.com   www.WTPLearn.com

"Improving WA through a Constitutional representative government"

Action Item: Step 2:

- Support a petition within your county to call a convention.
- See Exhibit A on page 113.

Chapter 6

The Quiet Rebellion

The Awakening of Counties

From 2A Sanctuaries, Invasion Declarations and the concern for County Sheriffs, we find the need for the most basic of elected offices being questioned.

Like a mother in the throes of labor, working through the challenges of the birthing process, or parents navigating the teenage years, America finds itself once again in the middle of a challenge, *what is the next iteration in governance for our country to include?* Our foundation, concepts as declared in our Declaration of Independence, the Constitution and Bill of Rights. What we are overlooking is how technology can be adapted to align more closely with the Truths as evidenced.

Truth is not something that can be discarded because someone declares the truth to be outdated. Truth is endearing and extends across all time. The Laws of Nature are literally what all nature must obey, including the truth attached to the laws of gravity, or laws dealing with energy.

Our Founding fathers identified how a Representative form of government was the ideal, ensuring that *as the Constitution was ratified, it was ratified* **not by a Popular vote of the States, but through a Representative vote.** States themselves, took it upon themselves to write State constitutions where none may have existed. Connecticut and Rhode Island both were operating under their Colonial Charters that had been granted in **1662** and **1663** respectively. Interesting how even with not having a state constitution, Connecticut became the primary sponsor for "The Great Compromise" which ensured a bicameral legislature federally and set the model for all States to do the same. The moral character of society was such, that all they wanted was a framework, or "Form of Government" to be created, so that all could follow, from the national to local levels. Not everything had to be codified, give us the framework and then let We the People do the rest. This was further indicated in the model where oaths of office are taken to support the Constitution, ensuring that process is followed, from our School Boards to our County, State and Federal offices.

Which then begs the question, why haven't counties done the same? Why haven't we followed more closely the federal model?

The work by ReclaimingTheRepublic.org lays out what may be the next critical iteration of 'We the People' as we exercise our right to self-governance. Counties provide the ideal set of conditions to ensure a resistance to "tyranny through interposition and petitions" (First Amendment).

From a hierarchy perspective, counties form the functional base of the republic, with states built above and the federal government with limited and defined rights on top. Without strong counties, the whole structure crumbles to "independent monarchs" in much the same way we see Washington State unfolding, as they are managing from the top down, even rewriting how sheriffs are to be elected.

Constitutional Compliance Committees:
- These are nonpartisan, citizen-formed groups to "examine government actions against the U.S. and state constitutions," auditing officials' oaths (Article VI) and petitioning for accountability (e.g., via Section **3** of the **14th** Amendment to remove violators).

- **The site provides templates for petitions**[42], declaring counties as "Constitutional Compliance Counties", with scripts for public hearings (e.g., South Dakota's HB-1082). Example: "Committees guide county legislators in drafting petitions to hold public servants accountable."

Real-world example: In Stevens County, WA (**2025**), a radio host pushed for the first such committee to lead "reclaiming the republic." Advocates like **Michelle Andres** distribute these at meetings, emphasizing: "It's not partisan—it's constitutional. It's our birthright. And it's time we reclaimed it." [43]

Writing/Adopting County Constitutions:

To formalize compliance, the site urges counties to "write or adopt" constitutions/charters as "Constitutional Counties", with limited documents that explicitly align local powers within federal/state frameworks, protecting sovereignty and enabling "Republic Review."

This isn't about granting new sovereignty but restoring historical autonomy eroded by modern violations. The **"Template for Building a Constitutional County"**[44] outlines steps: form a petition militia, drafting a charter limiting government to enumerated powers, and ratifying via citizen vote.

Chapter 7

Sheriffs, Commissioners, and the Chain of Command

The Last Constitutional Firewall

"The sheriff is the only constitutional officer who stands between the citizen and tyranny."

— Sheriff Richard Mack

"*The elected sheriff has been held to be the only officer in the U.S. Constitution who answers to counties, not states*". Yet we find in the admittance of Hawaii as a state, that they refused to incorporate the role of sheriff into their constitution or organized government.

To be clear though, neither the word Sheriff, nor the role of Sheriff, are mentioned in any part of the Constitution or the Bill of Rights. Yet the use of Sheriff does extend back into medieval England with the role of "shire reeve", or sheriff.

From the standpoint of brevity, we can learn that just because a role is not mentioned, does not mean that it is not relevant or that it is not needed. Core to the constitutional discussion is, **what do the people want?**

Hawaii had been governed with a top-down, centralized government as a result of being ruled by a king. The **13** original colonies had been authorized to form through charters granted by a king. The original colonies/states also had the benefit of coming out of **5** centuries of schooling under the Magna Carta which included the following:

79

The King of England provided:

Magna Carta 1215

Setting the precedent for constitutional limits on limiting power.

English Bill of Rights 1689

Provided a pivot toward civil liberties and the right to petition.

Then the Founding Fathers were inspired to create:

Articles of Confederation 1777

Initiated the confederated system of government

U.S. Constitution 1788

Pivoted from a confederation to centralized republicanism and representative government, enabling national unity while preserving state autonomy, becoming the template on Constitutional Form.

Bill of Rights 1791

The explicit safeguard to individual rights, becoming the global template for Form. Further clarifying and stabilizing understanding of rights held by 'We the People' and what was being entrusted to government.

While the French created:

The Rights of Man and of the Citizen 1789

Universalized republican ideas during the Revolution, spreading these concepts into the **19th** and **20th** centuries and beginning to permeate other cultures. Words on paper are not enough, as the French were to find out as they are now onto their Fifth Republic and perhaps **25** constitutional changes.

Americas constitution has enjoyed permanence, in large part because of its foundation on Truth, which includes a respect for that of Natures God. Following the concept of form, respect for God is best practiced locally, or within our counties, as well as in our churches.

Perhaps the roles within county governments (Sheriff, County Commissioner, Auditor, Coroner, and so forth), will only exist as long as the people choose to have them exist. Remember what Benjamin Franklin said, when asked what kind of government do we have. "A Republic if you can keep it."[45]

We have in many locales removed the County Coroner from being an elected office. Who is next? In some counties, it is the sheriff. As long as counties choose to be treated like the servant, the state will continue to take on greater Roles and Responsibilities.

Once again, the purpose of this exercise is to help all people find the strength to retain their voice as sovereign individuals, to ensure that the rights that have been fought for, for almost a millennium of time, can be retained. If you want to restore lower taxation, ensure greater transparency and accountability, then take the next step and pivot to Constitutional process within our Counties.

The firewall, if there is one, is the people.

Just like in the art of war, the best defense is an impenetrable wall. The same as the old school yard game, "Red Rover Red Rover, send Johnnie on over". For the schoolyard junkies that really knew how to play the game, you would interlock arms and hope for the best. On occasion someone would break an arm, but none-the-less we learned that our best defense started with ourselves taking responsibility.

People need to line up and get behind their county commissioners and their sheriffs, to lock arms and show to one another that your county will have a strong line of support. Likewise, counties need to unite and stand together to create a firewall against a state that wants to dismantle your authority. If allowed to go unchecked, states will do just like the federal government has been doing, growing unchecked to the point that we lose all peaceful constraint to control.

By virtue of the constitution, we have a line of command.

The Constitutional Chain of Command

We the People → Counties → State → Federal

1. **We the People**

   (as they recognize their rights from God)→

2. **Counties**

   (as the most local of government structures, via commissioners & sheriffs) →

3. **States**

   (as a collective of Counties, recognizing their limited rights and the representative process) →

Part III

The Solution

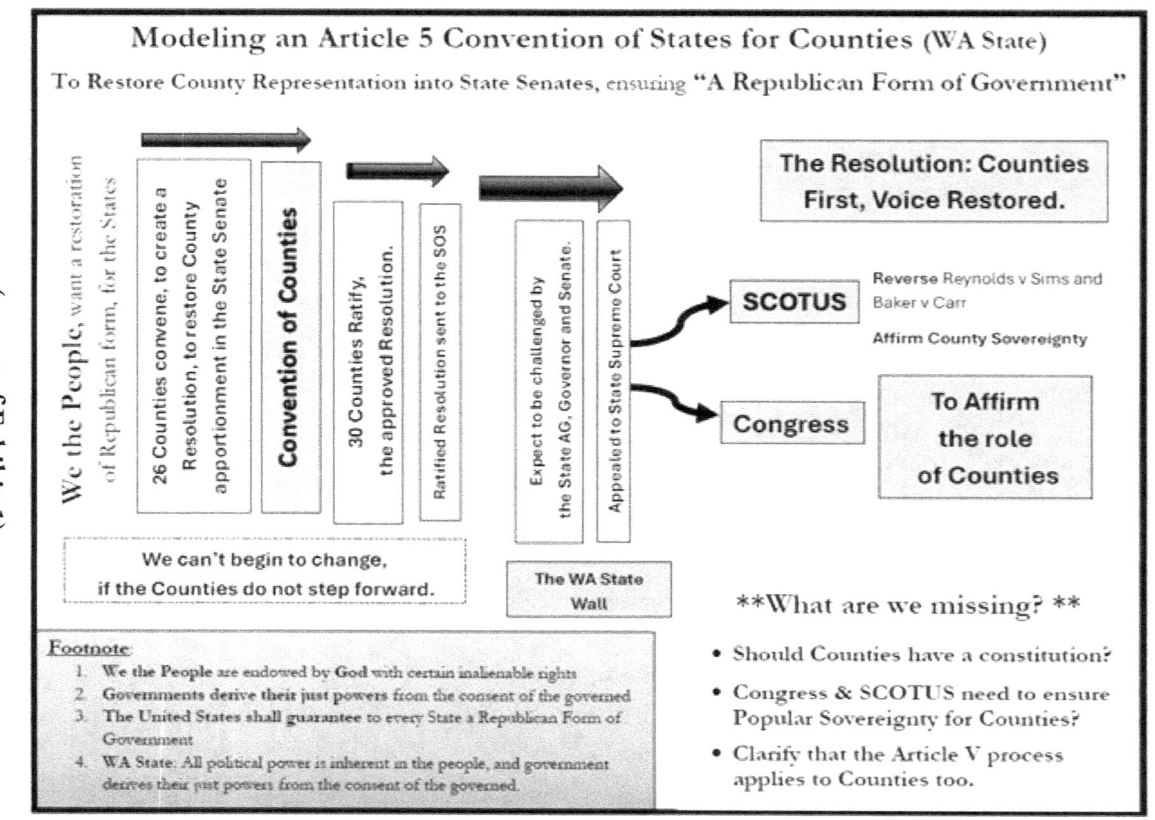

(repeat of Exhibit-1)

Chapter 8

The Convention of Counties

Legal, Historical, and Moral Justification

"The powers not delegated to the United States
by the Constitution, nor prohibited by it to the States,
are reserved to the States respectively,
or to the people."

— Tenth Amendment

The solution is not a new idea.

It is the original idea for correction, following form, <u>being applied at the state level.</u>

A Convention of Counties is simply Article V logic applied within the State: Just as states can call a convention to restrain the federal government, counties should be able to call a convention to restrain the states — and restore the republican form guaranteed by Article IV, Section 4, of the United States Constitution. The Washington State Constitution does not forbid this action, does yours?

If the Constitution does not forbid, then it must be a right reserved for the Citizens, as they are the ultimate holders of rights not delegated, and it is a right clearly identified within the U.S. Constitution and Declaration of Independence.

This is not rebellion.

This is enforcement.

The Legal Foundation:

Counties as Sovereign Political Communities

1.   **Historical Precedent and Representative votes**

State	Ratified Initial State Constitution Popular or Representative Vote
Delaware	Representative Vote
Pennsylvania	Representative Vote
New Jersey	Representative Vote
Georgia	Representative Vote
Connecticut	Representative Vote
Massachusetts	Popular Vote
Maryland	Representative Vote
Sourth Carolina	Representative Vote
New Hampshire	Representative Vote
Virginia	Representative Vote
New York	Representative Vote
North Carolina	Representative Vote
Rhode Island	Representative Vote

Exhibit 14

- **Ratification by Representative vote is how 12 of our 13 original states ratified their initial <u>state</u> constitutions.**

     Massachusetts was the only state to ratify by popular vote. If you might recall, this is the only state to split their vote on the **'Great Compromise'** in support of a bicameral system of government. Hard time deciding?

- **Ratification of the U.S. Constitution (1787–1791):**

  Ratifying of the U.S. Constitution was completed by representative vote in all states. Even Massachusetts elected delegates from their towns and districts to represent their vote for ratification, which was different from their State Constitution ratification.

  Through the process of county caucuses, we had such states as North Carolina, which further pushed for the guarantee of a Bill of Rights. Without the voice of counties, we may not have had a Bill of Rights.

  Note: that the use of towns was predominant within the New England states, where towns were the primary unit of self-governance.

- **New State Creation:**

  Enabling Act's were created by Congress, to identify how new states were to be admitted, with a simple requirement for constitutions to be written, in the example of Washington State, the Counties were to take the lead through convention to draft the subject constitution.

  Yet Congress began to progressively put additional requirements into the approval process, such as requiring the constitution to be ratified by a **popular** and <u>not a</u> **representative vote**, as were the original 13 states.

2. **The Federal Analogy**

   States are to the nation what counties are to the state. Article V allows **2/3** of states to propose amendments bypassing Congress.

By analogy, **2/3** of counties should be able to propose a restoration compact or amendment bypassing urban legislatures.

3. **The Guarantee Clause Enforcement**

    Article IV, Section **4**, is a positive duty on the federal government — and by extension, on the people when government fails.

    - Harlan in Reynolds dissent: Apportionment is not for courts. It's political — meaning for the people through political communities (counties).

4. **Moral Imperative**

    - When states become democracies instead of republics, they violate the contract.
    - Counties, as the "parents" of states, have the duty to correct.

"If the Guarantee Clause means anything, it means the people retain the ultimate power to enforce the form of government the Framers designed."

— Adapted from **Justice Harlan**

Action Item: (The one, two punch)

2/3 of the counties to pass a resolution, to call a convention:

Sample Resolution to be passed, See Exhibit B-1

Once the Convention is called,
keep it restrained and focused
on a single objective,
"Restoring the voice of counties
back into the State Senate".
Once the Convention is called,
the delegates need to agree to a Resolution
that can now be ratified by 3/4
of the counties within the state.

See Exhibit B-2

Chapter 9

How It Can Work

Step-by-Step Playbook

"If you can't describe what you are doing as a process, you don't know what you're doing."

— W. Edwards Deming

The Convention of Counties is not theory. It's a **process** — with timelines, templates, and proven steps.

Phase 1: The 90-Day Spark (Your County)

1. **Week 1–2: Become informed and Educate**
   - Host "Federal Analogy Night" at courthouse. Read from the Federalist papers mentioned in this book. Discuss the history of governance, pre-1964.
2. **Week 3–4: Build Support** (Using Exhibit-A)
   - Petition drive, secure signatures for your commissioners
   - Meet sheriff/commissioners privately.
3. **Week 5–12: Pass the Call** (Using Exhibit-B-1)
   - Present Model Resolution
   - Vote at commissioners meeting.
   - Goal: **2/3 of the counties**, call the convention, which begins the discussion for action.

Outcome:

Your county becomes the "Shackelford" for your state.

Phase 2: The Convention (Using Exhibit B-2)

For Washington State, this occurs with 26 of 39 counties, activating the process. Remember that not all States were present during the Philadelphia Convention.

- **Month 3:** have a proposed document for ratification, that Commissioners can readily support. Commissioners need to return to their counties, have open public meetings and push for ratification.
- **Month 3-6:** Secure ratifications by ¾ **of the counties**, which for Washington State is 30 counties, then record with the Secretary of State.

Phase 3: Acceptance by the State leadership -OR- into the courts and onto SCOTUS (the National Gathering)

- Push for legal process quickly, within the state courts
- Be prepared for seeking national support and an expedited hearing within SCOTUS
  - Draft restoration amendment or compact.
  - Options:
    1. Constitutional amendment (sent to states — but with county veto).
    2. Interstate compact binding participating states.

We need a single state to activate the process, followed by Counties and States to be friends of the Court.

As 500+ Counties create "Amicus curiae briefs" for the SCOTUS hearing, this will help to ensure that the cause for Restoring the voice of counties back into the state senates, becomes reality. This should also lend credible support for Counties to be recognized as to being duly entitled to the rights of Popular Sovereignty, and a restoration of Cooley's Doctrine.

Legal Safety Nets

Printz v. United States: States can't commandeer counties or states to enforce federal laws, specifically relating to background checks for handgun purchases.

- *No court has ever struck a county resolution on Guarantee Clause grounds. See **Pacific States Telephone & Telegraph v Oregon**, 223 U.S. 118 (**1912**)*
- *See **Luther v Borden**, 48 U.S. (7How.) (**1849**)*
- *See **Baker v. Carr**, 369 U.S. 186 (**1962**)*
- *See **Rucho v. Common Cause**, 588 U.S. (**2019**)*
- ***SCOTUS** rulings are reversed, often* [46]

Federalism, Counties and Early government

Are Local Governments Mere Creatures of the States? National Affairs www.nationalaffairs.com/publications/detail/are-local-governments-mere-creatures-of-the-state

Action Item:

Secure support from your County, even if the counties in your state have not called a convention yet, and forward a copy of your support to **Info@ConventionOfCounties.com**

Chapter 10

Reapportionment Done Right

Fixed County Senate Seats + Population-Based House
(5 model plans: WA, TX, FL, PA, generic)

"The senate… ought to be composed of representatives of the states as political societies."

— James Madison,
Constitutional Convention Notes

The fix is simple.

It's what we had for **175** years.

One house, **Representatives**, by population (**the people**).

One house, **Senate**, by fixed geography (**the counties**).

No more gerrymandering. No more urban wipeouts. <u>The Core Principle:</u>

- **House**: Apportioned by population (one person, one vote). Cities dominate — as they should for local issues.
- **Senate**: One or two seats per county (fixed geographies, no reapportionment). Rural voice permanent.

A federal analogy of what the Framers envisioned.

Model Plans: No need for constitutional amendments, 5 Real-World Examples:

1. **Washington State Model** (**39** counties, with **49** senate seats currently)

   - **Senate**: move to **39** seats — per state constitutional constraints, the senate is to have no less than 1/3 and no more than 1/2 the allocated seats of the house.

   - **House**: **98** seats —currently based on population apportionment. Decide, should each county have at minimum a single Representative, with more populated counties to be apportioned more seats (reduces the gerrymandering of districts). Or simply, continue with the current Legislative Districts, based on overall state boundaries.

   - **Result**: At minimum, the state senate is restored with **1** Senate seat per county. Rural veto restored, within the legislature, while also reducing the number of state senators from **49** to **39**.

   - **Pre-1964 Reality:** In **1889**, Washington had **35** Counties and **35** senate seats, with some counties receiving **3** senators and other counties combined for a single senator.

   - **Going forward:** Regarding the state senate, propose each county to have an equal voice of a single senator. If King County wants to subdivide into multiple counties, great. Population concentration will not be a consideration for senate seats, just as it was with the original **13** states.

2. **Texas Model** (**254** counties, **33** senate seats, currently)—*an idea for states with a high number of counties. Modeled after*

   - **Senate: 254** seats (***create Senate districts***, based on grouping).

- **House**: Current population model.
- Result: Harris County (Houston) dominates House but can't steamroll Senate. Border counties get equal voice.

3. **Florida Model** (**67** counties)
   - **Senate**: **67** seats — *1 per county.*
   - **House**: **120** population.
   - Result: Miami-Dade gets massive House power but can't override Panhandle on guns or water rights.

4. **Pennsylvania Model** (**67** counties)
   - **Senate**: **67** seats.
   - **House**: **203** population.
   - Result: Philadelphia can't dictate to rural coal counties.

5. **Generic National Template** (for any state)
   - **Senate**: **1** seat per county (or parish/district). Minimum **1**, maximum **2** for large states.
   - **House**: Pure population, with county floor (min **1** rep per county).

Sample-WA State, State Senate Seats: (Pre vs. Post Reynolds)

District Type	**Pre-1964** (1931)	**2024**	**Power Shift**
Rural (**Whitman**)	**1.3** seats	**.14** seats	**-89 %**
Urban (**King**)	**4** seats	**17** seats	**+325 %**

Why It Works
- **Ends judicial gerrymandering** (county lines are fixed by geography, for Senate seats)
- **Protects minorities** (geographic, cultural, economic)
- **Ensures Legislative dialogue** — exactly what republics do,

representatives working out issues

- **Protects, Checks and Balances**—reduces bad legislation and ensures "**Taxation with Representation**"
- **Protects personal freedoms**

Action Item:

Customize the model for your state.

Present to commissioners:

"This is what the Guarantee Clause ordered."

Chapter 11

Answering the Objections

"Gerrymandering," "Urban Rights", "Judicial Review" (Rebuttals anyone?)

"The Court's decisions… amount to nothing less than an exercise of the amending power by this Court."

— Justice Harlan

Critics will scream. Answer them with Truth.

Objection 1: "This is gerrymandering!"

Rebuttal: Fixed county lines are the opposite of gerrymandering.

- **Gerrymandering** = politicians drawing lines for ensuring power.
- **County lines** = historical, natural boundaries (rivers, mountains, communities).
- **Pre-1964**: Few referred to county senates as being "gerrymandered."
- **Post-1964**: Judges, with Legislative support, redraw every 10 years — that's gerrymandering.

Objection 2: "Urban voters get shortchanged!

Rebuttal: No — they dominate the House.

- **Cities and urban centers** already control population-based chambers.
- **Senate protects minorities** (rural, agricultural, energy-producing).

99

- **Framers**: "The senate prevents the tyranny of the majority." (Federalist 62)
- **Example**: California — L.A./SF would lose nothing in Assembly and yet couldn't dictate water to Central Valley.

Objection 3: "Courts will strike it down!"

Rebuttal: Several of the Warren SCOTUS decisions have been reversed, the time has come for the decisions relating to this problem to be reversed.

- **Guarantee Clause** is non-justiciable (Luther v. Borden, 1849). Political question for Congress/people.
- **Reynolds was wrong** — overruled the Constitution.
- **Counties act first**; courts chase.

Objection 4: "It's undemocratic!"

Rebuttal: Exactly. We're a representative republic.

- **Pure democracy** = mob rule.
- **Republic** = balanced, with brakes on majority.
- **Framers hated pure democracy** (Madison called it "spectacle of turbulence").

"the "One Person, One Vote" doctrine, manipulated the Fourteenth Amendment into funneling the general right of citizens to vote into the right to a particular kind of apportionment of state legislatures. Further mandating that apportionment be on a basis of population."

— Adapted from

Justice John Marshall Harlan II (1964)

This was Judicial Gerrymandering.

Action Item:

Prepare "Objection Rebuttal Sheet" (1-page). Hand to commissioners/media.

Determine what more can be said and prepare to engage in dialogue.

Chapter 12

Your County, Your Move

The 90-Day Plan to Pass the Call
(Letter to commissioners, petition drive, media kit)

"If I had one hour to save the world, I would spend fifty-five minutes defining the problem and only five minutes finding the solution."

— Albert Einstein

You don't need permission. You need a plan.
Here's the 90-day playbook any citizen can run.

Week 1–2: Define the Problem (Educate)
- **Host** "Federal Analogy Night" (courthouse or church).
- **Show**: Pre-1964 senate map vs. today.
- **Read**: Harlan dissent excerpt.
- **Goal**: 50 attendees.

Week 3–6: Build the Team
- **Recruit** 10 volunteers.
- **Petition** drive (template): "We call for a Convention of Counties to restore the Guarantee."
- **Goal**: Determine what you think your commissioners need to see.

Week 7–8: Engage Leaders
- Private meetings: Sheriff, commissioners (one-on-one).

- Present: Model Call resolution (Appendix B).
- Letter template: "Dear Commissioner, here's why your vote matters…"

Week 9–12: The Vote

- **Public hearing**: Pack the room (like Shackelford).
- **Speak**: 3-minute testimonies (veterans, ranchers, parents).
- **Vote**: Pass the Call.
- **Post-Vote**: Amplify
- **Press release** to local paper.
- **Share** on Social Media and with Convention of Counties
- **Tag state legislators**: "Your turn."
- **90-Day Checklist**

Week	Task	Done?
- 1–2	- Host education night	- [ ]
- 3–6	- Collect signatures	- [ ]
- 7–8	- Meet leaders	- [ ]
- 9–12	- Pass resolution	- [ ]

Action Item:

Start Week 1 today.

- This is your county. Make it the next Shackelford.

Chapter 13

A More Perfect Union, Again

America with 3,141 Sovereign Counties
What are the possibilities?

Is Americas secret weapon, her ingenuity and spirit to tinker, to explore new concepts. Why is it that these people left a mark on humanity, was it from their being closer to the resources, a recognition of living on what you have, or simply the ability to unleash human potential? In most cases, these individuals made contributions to society that improved productivity and provided improvements for all people to enjoy, globally. All had their grounding in rural America, the counties.

Look-up for yourself, some of the following, and see what you might learn:

- George Washington Carver (c 1864-1943)
- Thomas Edison (1847-1931)
- Philo Farnsworth (1906-1971)
- Garret Morgan (1877-1963)
- Henry Ford (1863-1947)
- Eli Whitney (1765-1825)
- Edward Huffaker (1856-1937)
- Alice H. Parker (1895-?)
- Will Allen (1949-present)
- Wright Brothers (Wilbur & Orville)
- John Deere (1804-1886)
- Cyrus McCormick (1809-1884)

- Frederick McKinley Jones (1893-1961)
- Lewis Howard Latimer (1848-1928)
- Henry Blair (1807-1860)
- Bernard Daines (1944-2014)
- Raymond Hanson (1923-2009)

These last two, the author knew personally and recognized how they contributed immensely to the improvement of life today, for people globally. The question for everyone, who do you know about that is not on the list? Who from your county, has contributed, have you? Expand a discussion.

Is it true that government today is one of the obstacles to innovation and business development? If this were felt more at the local level, and if local counties had greater control over process and their resources, would people be more inclined to be involved as we have seen in our history.

Better yet, are counties to be likened to the traditional garage. For **250** years the American Garage has quietly changed the world.

- **Hewlett-Packard** → the entire tech industry
- **Apple** → the smartphone in your pocket
- **Disney** → the happiest place on earth (started in a garage, scaled in Orange County)
- **Amazon** → started in Bezos's Bellevue garage
- **Google** → Susan Wojcicki's Menlo Park garage
- **Harley-Davidson**, **Mattel**, **Yankee Candle**, **MagLite**... the list is endless.

Two or three dreamers, zero permission, maximum freedom.

That tiny garage was the smallest unit still capable of total freedom in an increasingly regulated nation.

Now imagine that same freedom — but at county scale. 3,143 American counties.

Most have:

- More land than Silicon Valley ever had
- Better water, energy, and mineral resources than Dubai or Singapore ever dreamed of
- Millions of motivated citizens instead of 2–3 founders
- Existing airports, highways, courts, and schools

Counties are the garage on steroids.

We already have proof this works:

Miami-Dade County, FL (2021-2025) Mayor Suarez ran a one-man "unleash the county" experiment:

→ "How do I get to Miami?" tweets

→ Near-zero crypto regulation

→ Welcome mat for founders

Result: In <4 years Miami went from tech nowhere to hosting more crypto nodes than San Francisco. Thousands of founders and hundreds of funds moved in.

Orange County, CA (1950s–1980s)

Light zoning + defense money → invented the modern American suburb, Disneyland, and the semiconductor cluster that powered the PC revolution.

Travis County, TX (Austin)

Kept taxes and zoning sane → attracted Dell, Tesla Gigafactory, Samsung, Apple, and turned a sleepy college town into the hottest tech hub in America.

Three counties. Three explosions. All because someone got government out of the way.

A truly unleashed county beats even the wildest "charter city" fantasy in **10** out of **11** categories. It already has the roads, the courts, the hospitals, the people, and — most importantly — *the American spirit.*

The bottleneck has never been the land or the people. It has always been regulation and governance.

2026 can be the year we remove the chains.

Two simple, constitutional levers will do it:
1. **Restore real county representation in every state senate** (most states gutted it in the **1960s-70s** with "one man, one vote" rulings). **Counties must have their voice back.**
2. **Roll back the federal and state regulatory blanket** that smothers rural America.

Do this and the $36 trillion national debt becomes a rounding error. Counties will generate so much new wealth we'll pay it off the way we paid off World War II debt — with growth, not austerity.

However, it all starts with restoring the Representative voice to counties, to be exercised in their State Senate. Do this today, and this capacity to unleash the greatest economic expansion, begins today as well.

This is not about a single person taking action, but about the collective group of "We the People", finding our voice and ensuring that our voice is heard today, and for generations to come as we Restore the voice of Rural America, back into their State Senates. Let the counties compete and innovate for Americas future.

Chapter 14

Final Thoughts

Truth Restored

As I was listening to the podcast "**Google, The AI Company**", by the team at Acquired, the thought occurred that another example of a great pivot in business, occurred when Jensen Huang, recognized the Big Bang moment of Artificial Intelligence as Geoff Hinton, Alex Krzyzewski and Ilya Sutskever used an "off the shelf" NVIDIA GeForce GTX **580** gaming card for computers in a technology competition.

This revolutionary pivot with NVIDIA's GPUs—starting with CUDA in **2006-2007**—transformed AI by repurposing existing parallel-processing hardware (originally built for gaming graphics) into a scalable, accessible platform that dramatically accelerated deep learning. This unlocked exponential progress: models that once took weeks to train could now run in hours, enabling breakthroughs like **AlexNet** in **2012** and the rapid scaling to today's massive generative AI systems, democratizing innovation so that researchers, startups, and companies could experiment at unprecedented speed and scale without prohibitive costs or delays.

This same principle of **repurposing an underutilized, already-deployed resource** to supercharge a larger system applies directly to counties in American governance. Counties, like pre-CUDA GPUs, were designed for a more localized "niche" function—administering everyday community needs such as records, health, elections, and land use—yet they represent stable, granular geographic units with deep historical roots in representing diverse local interests.

In the founding era, many state legislatures (especially upper houses) drew representation from counties or groups of counties to balance area-based and population-based power, echoing the federal Senate's state-equality model and preserving popular sovereignty close to home. The founders also supported the underlying tenants of the Cooley Doctrine, since this reinforced the ideas associated with Representative Government, along with respecting the building blocks of local government.

Over time, as centralized progressive reforms shifted authority upward—nationalizing policy through bureaucracies, mandates, and expert-led agencies—counties became sidelined taking a back seat to higher representation, much like GPUs were confined to graphics before CUDA "unlocked" their potential.

Re-empowering counties—by using county boundaries as hard constraints in redistricting, basing state senate districts on county clusters with proportional or multi-member systems, or giving counties stronger roles in state initiatives—could similarly accelerate and democratize representative government. It would restore granular accountability to "We the People" at the local level, countering seniority-protected centralization, reducing gerrymandering distortions, and amplifying diverse voices without reinventing the entire system from scratch. We the People, need to insist on a return to the tenants of Cooley's Doctrine along with recognized support for Popular Sovereignty. We the People, organized and created this government, we created the laws through our representatives, we have a right and responsibility to clarify the underlying tenants of our governing structure and not leave it to the discretion of a select group of legal scholars. The judiciary was to be the weakest arm of government, and yet it is growing into becoming the strongest.

Just as CUDA turned a gaming tool into the engine of the AI revolution, strategically leveraging counties could reignite the original promise of popular sovereignty, making democracy more responsive, scalable, and truly bottom-up once again.

As We the people, become more civically involved, and understand what was intended, we will then receive in the end, fulfillment of the guarantee, provided for in our United States Constitution; that

"The United States shall guarantee to every State in this Union a Republican Form of Government."

As **Benjamin Franklin** stated when asked what kind of government do we have?

"A republic, if you can keep it".

Now is the time for states to insist on the restoration of the Republican Form, we were guaranteed, by calling a Convention of Counties to restore County Representation back into their State Senate.

Appendix A

The Petition

Step 1

Support for Convention of Counties

We, your constituents of ___________________________ County hereby notify you of our support for the calling of a "Convention of Counties", a concept that is modeled after an **Article 5, Convention of States.**

By our signature below, we are asking you to support this "Convention of Counties" to reapportion the Washington **State Senate to have equal representation from all 39 counties.**

Further, we support the election of the Senator upon ratification of agreement by 30 of the counties. **This office of State Senator is to represent the interests of the ENTIRE county.**

We support this Convention being called as soon as possible, so that we can have the representation as guaranteed in the U.S. Constitution.

Signature (As on voter registration)	Print Name	Address where you are registered	City	ZIP Code
1 Matt Hawkins	Matt Hawkins	200 S. Washington	Any	00000
2				
3				
4				
5				
6				
7				
8				
9				
10				
11				
12				
13				
14				
15				
16				
17				
18				
19				
20				

ConventionOfCounties.com   www.WTPLearn.com

"Improving WA through a Constitutional representative government"

Citizens to sign a 1st Amendment Petition, to request their Commissioners to take action.

The County Resolution to Call the Convention

Pass a county resolution, to call a convention:

Sample, designed for Washington State

RESOLUTION NO. ___

A RESOLUTION CALLING FOR A CONVENTION OF COUNTIES WITHIN THE STATE OF WASHINGTON TO RESTORE COUNTY REPRESENTATION IN THE STATE SENATE CONSISTENT WITH A 'REPUBLICAN FORM OF GOVERNMENT'

WHEREAS, the Declaration of Independence affirms that *governments are instituted among the people, deriving their just powers from the consent of the governed*, and that the people retain the right to alter or reform systems of government that become destructive of their ends; and

WHEREAS, the Constitution of the United States assures that all states entering into the Union of States, are to enjoy the same privileges and benefits as the original 13 states, (Article IV, Section 3); and

WHEREAS, the Constitution of the United States guarantees to every State in this Union a *Republican Form of Government* (Article IV, Section 4), a form historically understood at the Founding to include balanced representation, and structural restraints against consolidation of power; and

WHEREAS, the federal Constitution itself was framed through compromise between popular representation and representation of distinct political communities, resulting in a **bicameral legislature**, with one chamber representing the people proportionally and the other representing constituent political units (the States) on a fixed and equal basis, known historically as the **Great Compromise**; and

WHEREAS, this model of bicameralism was adopted by the States, and

WHEREAS, counties are among one of the oldest and most durable political subdivisions in American governance, historically serving not merely as administrative districts but as expressions of localized popular sovereignty through which the people govern themselves; and

WHEREAS, the scholarly and historical analysis *(Are Local Governments Mere Creatures…)* demonstrates that local governments have long functioned as constitutional instruments of self-rule, not merely as subordinate agencies of centralized authority; and

WHEREAS, the progressive consolidation of legislative power at the state level, combined with population-based apportionment of both legislative chambers, has diminished the voice of the people through their counties as distinct political communities within the State of Washington; and

WHEREAS, this consolidation has weakened governance within the State, reduced structural checks on centralized authority, and impaired the ability of rural and geographically distinct counties to participate meaningfully in the legislative process; and

WHEREAS, the Constitution of the State of Washington is silent as to any prohibition on counties assembling in convention for the purpose of petitioning, proposing, or recommending structural reforms consistent with republican government and popular sovereignty; and

WHEREAS, peaceful, deliberative conventions have been a historically recognized means by which the American people have expressed sovereign authority, proposed reforms, and corrected structural defects in government, including but not limited to the Federal Convention of 1787; and

WHEREAS, nothing in the Constitution of the United States forbids the people of a State, acting through their counties, from assembling to deliberate upon and ensure reforms to their internal structure of representation, provided such reforms remain consistent with a republican form of government and the supremacy of federal law;

NOW, THEREFORE, BE IT RESOLVED:

SECTION 1.

That the Board of County Commissioners hereby affirms that **counties are foundational political communities**, not merely administrative units, and that their meaningful representation is essential to a republican form of government.

SECTION 2.

That this Board calls for the convening of a **Convention of Counties within the State of Washington**, composed of duly selected delegates from each county, for the limited and peaceful purpose of deliberating upon structural reforms to restore county-based representation in the State Senate.

SECTION 3.

That the Convention of Counties shall examine and consider proposals whereby the **State Senate will be restored back to being apportioned by fixed county boundaries**, so as to reflect the constitutional logic of bicameralism embodied in the Great Compromise— balancing population-based representation with representation of political communities.

SECTION 4.

That any recommendations or proposals emerging from such a Convention shall be **returned to the county for ratification**.

SECTION 5.

That this Resolution is not an act of secession, nullification, or defiance of lawful authority, but a **1st Amendment Petition** to **peaceful assertion of popular sovereignty**, undertaken in the spirit of constitutional process, historical continuity, and self-government.

ADOPTED this ___ day of ________, 2026
by the Board of County Commissioners of __________ County, Washington.

_________________________ Commissioner

_________________________ Print Name

_________________________ Commissioner

_________________________ Print Name

_________________________ Commissioner

_________________________ Print Name

The Document to be Ratified by 30 Counties. (WA)

Proposed idea:

AGREEMENT TO RESTORE COUNTY REPRESENTATION INTO THE SENATE for the STATE OF WASHINGTON,

Restoring County-Based Representation in the State Senate Consistent with a Republican Form of Government

WHEREAS, the County Commissioners for the State of Washington convened a Convention of Counties to restore the apportioning of the Washington State Senate back to county districts; and

WHEREAS the County Commissioners desire to follow the model as provided in the U.S. Senate of equally apportioning the Senate body by fixed boundaries, the counties, by providing equal representation from all 39 counties, with the election of one Senator per county to represent the interests of the entire county; and

WHEREAS this agreement has been ratified by 30 of the 39 counties; and

WHEREAS, the Resolution calling for a Convention of Counties affirms that counties are foundational political communities essential to a republican form of government; and

WHEREAS, this agreement builds upon the principles outlined in the Petition and Resolution to restore the voice of counties in the State Senate, ensuring meaningful participation of distinct political communities in the legislative process; and

WHEREAS, the current population-based apportionment of both legislative chambers has diminished the representation of counties as sovereign political units, contrary to the historical model of bicameralism embodied in the Great Compromise of the U.S. Constitution; and

WHEREAS, this amendment seeks to restore the Washington State Constitution with the guarantee of a republican form of government under Article IV, Section 4 of the U.S. Constitution, by providing fixed and equal county representation in the Senate; and

WHEREAS, this amendment is proposed through the deliberative process of the Convention of Counties, as a peaceful assertion of popular sovereignty and self-government;

NOW, THEREFORE, BE IT RATIFIED BY THE CONVENTION OF COUNTIES OF THE STATE OF WASHINGTON:

That the following clarification to the Constitution of the State of Washington be adopted, recognizing that ratification by at least 30 of the 39 counties through their respective Boards of County Commissioners or by a majority vote of the qualified electors in each county has occurred:

CLARIFICATION AND ORDER OF BUSINESS

Article II of the Constitution is clarified as follows:

SECTION 2. HOUSE OF REPRESENTATIVES AND SENATE. The house of representatives shall be composed of ninety-eight members. The senate shall be composed of thirty-nine members, one elected from each county.

SECTION 43. REDISTRICTING (b) The senate shall be apportioned into thirty-nine senatorial districts consisting of the thirty-nine counties of the state as they exist at the time of redistricting, with each county constituting one district and electing one senator, regardless of population. Adjustments to senatorial district boundaries shall only be made in the event of changes to county boundaries as provided by law. (d) This section shall supersede any conflicting provisions in Article II regarding the apportionment of the senate.

RATIFICATION: This clarification to Senate apportionment shall be ratified upon approval by at least thirty (30) of the thirty-nine (39) counties in the State of Washington, as evidenced by resolutions adopted by their respective Boards of County Commissioners, or alternatively by a majority vote of the qualified electors in at least thirty (30) counties at a special election called for that purpose, as determined by the County. Upon ratification, the amendment shall be certified by the Secretary of State and incorporated as policy for Washington State.

ADOPTED by the Convention of Counties this ____ day of _________, 2026.

Reynolds v. Sims

Full Text: Justice Harlan's Dissent in Reynolds v. Sims + Dirksen Amendment

Short review, Wikisource: Reynolds v. Sims/Dissent Harlan - Wikisource, the free online library

Constitution Center: Reynolds v. Sims | Constitution Center

American History, the video: Bing Videos

The Full Case: Reynolds v. Sims | 377 U.S. 533 (1964) | Justia U.S. Supreme Court Center

1787–1964 Historical Timeline + Pre-Reynolds State

Senate Maps Timeline:

- **1787**: Connecticut Compromise.

All States are entitled to the same rights as the original 13 states.

- **1788–1791: Ratification <u>by county</u>**

Legal encroachment begins

- **1860:** 44 out of 45 State Senates apportioned based on Counties.
- **1889**: Washington Enabling Act — county senate.
- **1950**: Progressive policies further impacting

SCOTUS Intervenes

- **1962**: Engel v. Vitale distraction.
- **1964**: Reynolds coup. ***All state senate seats*** *are apportioned by population.*
- **1965**: Dirksen amendment fails by 7 votes.

All States lose Representative Government

- **2024–2025**: Counties begin to wake up, to restore Representation lost

The Ultimate: A National Amendment

A Constitutional Amendment to Restore a true bicameral system back into our State legislatures, and to ensure that "WE the People" and our "counties", are guaranteed the privileges of Popular Sovereignty.

PROPOSED AMENDMENT TO
THE CONSTITUTION OF THE UNITED STATES

To Ensure **Republican Form of Government** in the States by ensuring Representation of Political Subdivisions in State Senate Legislatures

WHEREAS, the Constitution of the United States guarantees to every State in this Union a Republican Form of Government (Article IV, Section 4), historically understood to include balanced representation (House and Senate) and structural restraints against the consolidation of power; and

WHEREAS, the federal Constitution embodies the Great Compromise, with the Senate apportioned equally among the States as fixed political units by State boundaries, balancing population-based representation in the House of Representatives; and

WHEREAS, this model of bicameralism should extend to the States to preserve the voice of distinct political communities within each State; and

WHEREAS, counties, as extensions of "We the People," are to enjoy the benefits of Cooley's doctrine of inherent local self-government and the principle of Popular Sovereignty, serving as foundational expressions of localized authority and not merely administrative subdivisions; and

WHEREAS, population-based apportionment in both chambers of many State legislatures has diminished the representation of counties and other fixed political subdivisions, weakening checks on centralized power and impairing meaningful participation by geographically distinct communities; and

WHEREAS, this proposed amendment seeks to align State governments with the republican principles of the federal model, enshrined as a Guarantee within the U.S. Constitution wherein all States are guaranteed a Republican Form of Government, which should ensure States the right to apportion one legislative chamber by fixed boundaries such as counties, through Representative vote upholding popular sovereignty.

NOW, THEREFORE, BE IT PROPOSED:
That the following article is proposed as an amendment to the Constitution of the United States, which shall be valid to all intents and purposes as part of the Constitution when ratified by the legislatures of three-fourths of the several States, or by conventions in three-fourths thereof, as the one or the other mode of ratification may be proposed by the Congress:

AMENDMENT [Next Sequential Number, e.g., XXVIII]
SECTION 1. To fulfill the guarantee of a Republican Form of Government, each State may apportion one chamber of its legislature, preferably the upper house or senate, on the basis of equal representation

from fixed political subdivisions, such as counties or equivalent units, following the model of equal apportionment in the United States Senate among the States and based on Representative vote.

SECTION 2. Such apportionment shall provide equal membership per subdivision, elected to represent the interests of the entire subdivision, with terms and qualifications as determined by State law, provided that it maintains staggered elections where applicable and respects the principles of one person, one vote in the other legislative chamber.

SECTION 3. Nothing in this Amendment shall prohibit States from using population-based apportionment in one chamber, nor shall it mandate changes to existing State constitutions without the consent of the people through their State processes, but it affirms the right of States to adopt or restore subdivision-based representation to enhance balanced governance, and affirms the right of Counties as enjoying the right of Popular Sovereignty and the principles of Cooley's Doctrine.

This amendment shall take effect two years after the date of ratification.

Recommended Reading & Organizations Books

- A Patriots History of the United States
- Why Counties Matter, By Reclaiming the Republic
- Nullification by Thomas Woods
- The Doctrine of the Lesser Magistrates by Matthew Trewhella
- Federalist Papers (62, 39)
- The Common Sense Guide to American History, by Anders Odegard

Organizations:
- Convention of Counties (Restoring Truth) (https://ConventionOfCounties.com)
- Reclaiming the Republic
- Constitutional Sheriffs and Peace Officers Association (CSPOA)
- Hillsdale College

Resources abound for Constitutional understanding. However here are a few resources for taking action:

Color versions of the charts will be updated at:

https://ConventionOfCounties.com

Constant Contact:

Substack: ConventionOfCounties.substack.com

WTPlearn's Substack | Substack

X: @COC1776 and @matthawkins4aud
Email: info@ConventionOfCounties.com

**The Beginning of creating Constitutional Counties. Please visit:
www.ReclaimingTheRepublic.org**

You will find within this site key resources relating to the
use of Constitutional Compliance Committees within
Counties, as well as model 1st Amendment Petitions,
to begin the process of restoring a more constitutional
compliant government at all levels of government.
Here you will find a clear solution for building a
Constitutional County.

Republic Review is a process, built around the idea
of audits as understood by Madison and Jefferson, to
ensure compliance with Constitutional process.

About the Author

Matt Hawkins is a dedicated husband, father of **10**, grandfather, and lifelong resident of Washington State, where he has been married to his wife Paula for over **37** years. Raised in a large family of eight children in the beautiful Pacific Northwest, Matt's early life was shaped by strong community ties, including participation in schooling, sports, scouting, and church activities. These experiences instilled in him core values of resourcefulness, observation, faith in God, and patriotism—values reinforced during America's Bicentennial era and mentored by a generation influenced by World War II veterans and the Great Depression.

Growing up amid "garage industries" and hands-on tinkering fostered a practical, problem-solving mindset that has carried through his life. Matt witnessed firsthand the economic challenges of recent decades, from the Vietnam War's aftermath and oil embargoes to high interest rates, the Savings and Loan Crisis, telecom and tech busts, and the Great Recession. A pivotal awakening came in **2018**, as he observed politicians openly embracing socialist policies, prompting him to investigate election integrity and the feasibility of audits.

This led to his **2024** campaign for Washington State Auditor, where he advocated for transparency, accountability, and fiscal responsibility to restore trust in government. Though he did not win the general election, the experience highlighted systemic issues around representation and the erosion of constitutional principles. As a former national consultant, Matt delivered actionable results for clients who prioritized outcomes over reports, applying business management principles to drive efficiency and cut waste. This experience of civic engagement, combined with the consulting past, opened up the reality that the problems identified could be solved, now, by restoring counties back into their state senates.

A family man who has raised 10 children, Matt remains deeply concerned about the state of education, particularly the lack of constitutional literacy among younger generations. He founded **Restoring Truth** as a platform to revive historical awareness, promote faithful adherence to constitutional governance, and to ensure that future generations inherit a debt-free republic rooted in representation, accountability, and timeless American values.

Matt's work seeks not merely to recount history for its own sake, but making it urgently relevant and actionable—empowering citizens to restore transparent, limited government that honors God, country, and individual responsibility.

This book offers the simplest, lowest-cost keys to putting all states back on the path to prosperity. The investment is minimal; the rewards are immense. Roll up your sleeves—we all have work to do.

This is not about the author; it is about each of us stepping up. Engage your county commissioners, pass the necessary resolutions, and ratify them across your state's counties.

Counties: we have a nation to save.

The Pathway for restoring the voice of counties, utilizing a Convention of Counties.

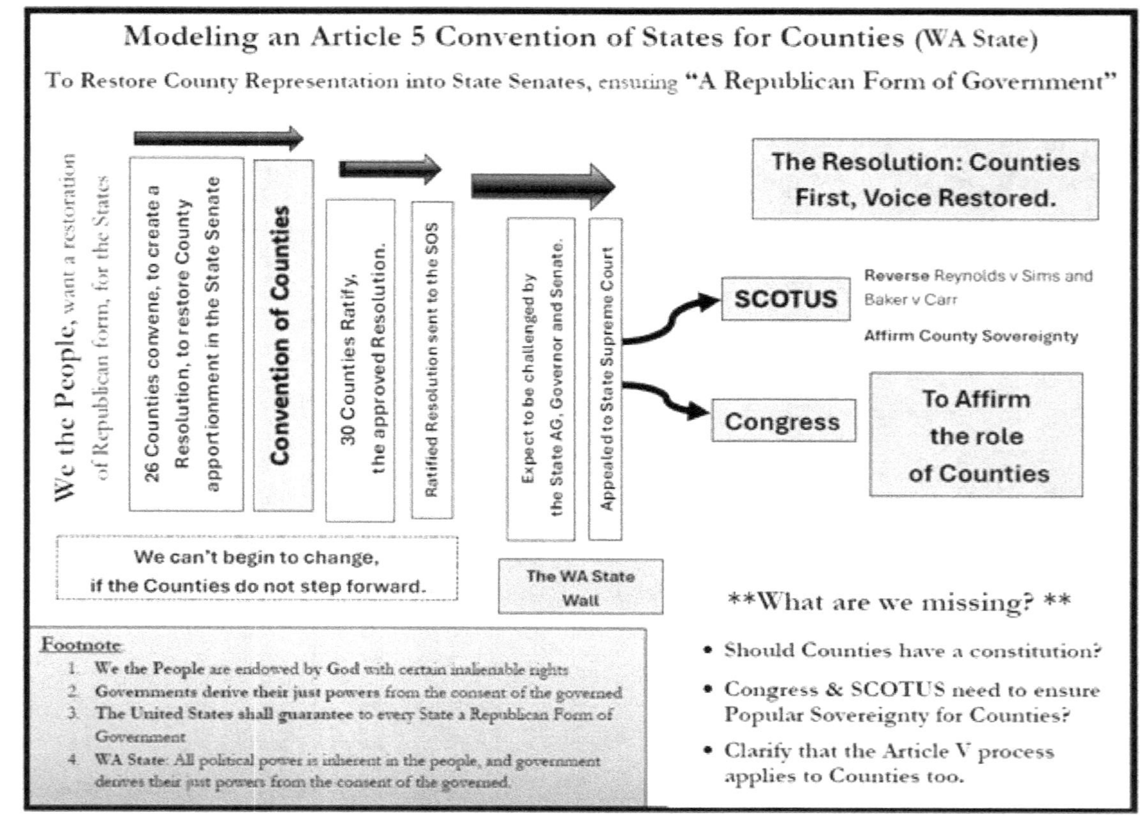

Questions to Consider

How can this be adapted to your State?
How can you engage students in history class,
to engage in the discussion?

*Perhaps it is time to re-engage a discussion within our churches, not
from a standpoint of political polarity, but from creating a deeper
understanding of how being more civically involved will improve our
communities.*

***Churches**: if the Constitution was divinely inspired, then
**how can we ensure the light that shines,
benefits all humanity?***

***Religious adherents,** and those that may not attend church: Do you
enjoy the religious and other freedoms the Constitution provides, do you
want to ensure this for future generations?*

***Atheists & Agnostics:** if America has benefited all of humanity, as a
result of the inspired direction of our Founding Fathers, then should we
not build on this legacy and ensure a Representative Form of government
is maintained, at all levels?*

If you are unsure, contact the author at:
info@ConventionOfCounties.com
For updates and insights,
Substack: https://conventionofcounties.substack.com
For updates and insights through **Constant Contact**:
bit.ly/4qNV5BB
Both newsletters are free for people that want to learn more.

Endnotes

1   53 Texas counties have now declared an invasion at southern border | The Highland County Press

2   Washington state sues Adams County to stop illegal federal immigration enforcement | Washington State

3   Can Munchausen by proxy be related to Munchausen by Olympia, if Munchausen by Olympia is in relation to State Government exhibiting the same characteristics. And compared with Grok, https://x.com/i/grok/share/Zk242UXBTtg9rOkoH1hCe4J5d

4   Munchausen Syndrome by Proxy: Symptoms, Causes, Treatment, Warnings

5   See Article XIII of the Articles of Confederation, "And the Articles of this Confederation shall be inviolably observed by every State, **and the Union shall be perpetual; nor shall any alteration at any time hereafter be made in any of them; unless such alteration be agreed to in a Congress of the United States, and be afterwards confirmed by the legislatures of every State**."

6   https://www.senate.gov/artandhistory/history/common/briefing/Constitution_Senate.htm

7   https://constitutioncenter.org/the-constitution/articles/article-iv/clauses/42

8   www.dirksencenter.org/wp-content/uploads/The-Long-Hard-Furrow.pdf **and** https://www.americanrhetoric.com/speeches/everettmdirksencivilrightsbillspeechfeb1964.htm **and** https://

www.loc.gov/exhibits/civil-rights-act/multimedia/everett-dirksen.html

9   Federalist #62, https://founders.archives.gov/documents/Hamilton/01-04-02-0212 **Federalist #63**, https://founders.archives.gov/documents/Hamilton/01-04-02-0213

10 Apportionment of State Legislatures 1776-1920.pdf

11 https://en.wikisource.org/wiki/Reynolds_v._Sims/Dissent_Harlan

12 https://constitutioncenter.org/the-constitution/supreme-court-case-library/reynolds-v-sims **and** https://law2.umkc.edu/faculty/projects/ftrials/conlaw/ReynoldsvSims.html

13 https://www.jstor.org/stable/1110287

14 https://www.usconstitution.net/founding-fathers-on-civic-duty-2/

15 https://www.virginialawreview.org/wp-content/uploads/2020/12/Kilberg_Book.pdf

16 https://www.nationalaffairs.com/publications/detail/are-local-governments-mere-creatures-of-the-state

17 https://teachingamericanhistory.org/resource/fafd-stagetwo/

18 https://www.molloy.edu/about/community-outreach/history-of-long-island/local-government

19 https://www.nvnaco.org/wp-content/uploads/History-and-Overview-of-County-Government-n-the-U.S.-NACo.pdf and https://k12database.unc.edu/wp-content/uploads/sites/31/2012/05/CountiesMunicipalities10.pdf

20 Avalon Project - Ratification of the Constitution by the State of Virginia; June 26, 1788

21 Avalon Project - Ratification of the Constitution by the State of New York; July 26, 1788

22 leg.wa.gov/media/dh5nkrlu/organic.pdf

23 First Washington Constitutional Convention convenes in Walla Walla on June 11, 1878. - HistoryLink.org

24 leg.wa.gov/about-the-legislature/history-of-the-legislature/enabling-act/?showall=false

25 Convention of 1836 - Wikipedia

26 Bing Videos and see commentary U.S. Constitution: What does popular sovereignty really mean? | Opinion – Deseret News

27 https://teachingamericanhistory.org/document/letter-to-john-adams-2/

28 https://www.nationalaffairs.com/publications/detail/are-local-governments-mere-creatures-of-the-state

29 Aristotle: 'Republics decline into democracies and democracies degenerate into despotisms.' — The Socratic Method

30 www.constitutionus.com/constitution/the-great-compromise/

31 uscode.house.gov/view.xhtml?path=/prelim@title25/chapter14&edition=prelim also see the original Act www.loc.gov/collections/united-states-statutes-at-large/about-this-collection/

32 https://www.theglobalstatistics.com/average-gas-prices-by-state/

33 https://www.washingtonpolicy.org/library/docLib/Myers-Climate-Spending-Waste.pdf

34 https://www.msn.com/en-us/politics/government/waste-of-the-day-washington-pays-for-homeless-crisis/ar-AA1N5i0o

35 https://www.seattletimes.com/seattle-news/politics/voters-said-yes-to-tough-new-gun-law-at-least-12-county-sheriffs-say-they-wont-enforce-it/

36 https://www.northcountrypublicradio.org/news/npr/696400737/when-sheriffs-won-t-enforce-the-law

37 https://cspoa.org/

38 https://www.fairus.org/sites/default/files/2018-05/Sanctuary-Report-FINAL-2018.pdf

39 https://wacities.org/docs/default-source/event-materials/munibudget/05budgetworkshoppropertytax101.pdf?sfvrsn=3b2c2b4f_1

40 https://reason.com/volokh/2024/01/12/federal-court-upholds-biological-sex-based-access-rule-for-school-restrooms/

41 https://cursus.edu/en/33572/the-urban-exodus-how-to-understand-the-repopulation-of-the-countryside

42 http://www.reclaimingtherepublic.org/petitions.html

43 https://loudoun-liberty.org/spotlight-on-citizen-action-michelle-andres/

44 http://www.reclaimingtherepublic.org/CC.html

45 https://www.nps.gov/articles/000/constitutionalconvention-september17.htm

46 List of overruled United States Supreme Court decisions - Wikipedia

* 9 7 9 8 2 3 4 0 1 0 9 8 8 *